Modern LACE DESIGNS

Veronica Sorenson

B.T. Batsford Ltd, London

ISBN 0 7134 4206 9

Filmset by Latimer Trend & Company, Plymouth
and printed in Great Britain by
Butler & Tanner Ltd, Frome, Somerset

for the publishers
B. T. Batsford Ltd.
4 Fitzhardinge Street
London W1H 0AH

Contents

Acknowledgements

I would like to express my thanks to the following people, without whom this book would never have been written. To Betty Maynard, who inveigled me into accompanying her to lacemaking classes at the North Havering College of Adult Education. To Valerie Harris for initiating me into the mysteries of the craft. To Jeanne Snow and her continuous encouragement of my work, even of the more outrageous designs and ideas. To Gwen Hatwell and her invaluable help in proofreading the typescript. To Dick Chenery, without whose photographic expertise I should have been lost. And lastly, my heartfelt gratitude to my husband who has supported me throughout this venture and my daughters who have suffered deprivation of dinners for so many months.

1 Bobbin lacemaking in the 1980s

The lace revival

It seems incredible that between the First and Second World Wars lacemaking almost became extinct and yet, now, in the 1980s, the revival has become so widespread that there are few British Local Authorities who do not offer at least one Adult Education weekly class in the subject. There are also specialised residential crash courses of up to one week offered by the English Lace School at Rockbeare near Exeter and a number of other craft-orientated Adult Education establishments.

When the latest boom in lacemaking commenced in the 1950s, there were few text books to assist the lacemaker. There had never been a need for instruction manuals as such because the knowledge of the craft was passed from mother to daughter verbally or from direct practical tuition in the lace schools. Anyway, books would have been of little use to the lacemakers of old as rarely could any of them read or write.

The number of publications over the last decade has made up for this shortage and every type of lace has been covered. This book, therefore, makes no pretensions to be an instruction manual nor does it focus on the history of lace or the reproduction of traditional patterns which are both areas that have been well covered in other works for the beginner. It is presumed that the lacemaker working the patterns in this book has a good knowledge of basic stitches and techniques and now wishes to experiment with them. It contains a collection of designs that are slightly different from the usual in that colour may be used, or the stitches may be combined in an unusual way, or the project may be of mammoth proportions.

The modern lacemaker

Originally lacemaking was a craft handed down from mother to daughter and it was later taught to young children in schools to enable them to earn a living from lacemaking. It is, needless to say, impossible to make a living at lacemaking in the 1980s. More especially in these times of economic recession and unemployment. Indeed, working at a rate of 200 pins per hour (fast by any standards) and for 50 pence per hour (a fraction of the rate demanded by the Trade Unions) a narrow Bucks Point edging, barely one inch wide, can be produced at a cost of £12 per metre. This is without regard to the cost of the initial materials and the time spent preparing prickings and bobbins. Compare this to the machine-made look-alike at a few pence per metre and, to the uninitiated, what does it matter that the hand-made lace is virtually indestructible. Lacemaking has become a truly international pastime. Once, when a lacemaker's livelihood depended on her output, patterns were jealously guarded so that no one else would be able to reproduce an identical piece of work, and designs became very insular. Thus, the patterns of a region became known only to those living locally. But, nowadays, these secrets are being shared with others and the idea that only people who lived in Buckinghamshire, for example, could make Bucks Point lace has disappeared.

Even the language of lacemaking became diverse due to the insular nature of the lacemakers. For example: the workers are called weavers in some districts; cloth stitch is also known as linen stitch; plaits, braids, brides and bridges are all words for the same thing; and tallies are also known as leaves, plaits or leadwork according to the region in which the lacemaker resides.

Once the basic knowledge of technique has been grasped, however, and the code of pattern writing has been understood, it is possible to reproduce laces from other countries without knowledge of the written language or the vocabulary.

The lacemaker attempting the fan in this book will discover Bruges techniques combined with Bucks Point and Torchon stitches, thus giving an attractive overall design with a slight difference.

Lacemaking may not be a feasible way of earning a living in the 1980s, but its popularity as a craft is increasing all the time, and with every age-group. Age means very little in the modern Adult Education class. Teenagers work side by side with senior citizens in total harmony. It is a wonderful way of breaking the age barrier and bringing different sections of the community together. Physical infirmities are no deterrent in this craft either. Indeed, it can give a wheelchair-bound person a new lease of life. Arthritic hands can often hold and move bobbins when they have difficulty in manoeuvring a sewing needle or knitting pins. Also, it is a most therapeutic craft for those with problems allied to the stress of modern living, and it is as good at relaxing tension as any drug the doctors can prescribe.

Adapting lace for the 'eighties

Bobbin lacemaking has now been in existence for almost 500 years. It is very important for the future of the craft that this generation designs patterns to encourage our young people to want to learn to make lace. They, after all, will be our lacemakers of the future. The youth of today has not, in general, the patience to spend the many hours necessary to produce a piece of the finest lace as worked in days past when the pace of life was so much slower and time of far less importance. In these days of 'instant' everything, young people want to be able to produce something that is quick to make but that is still striking.

The beautiful delicacy of the antique laces can never be achieved nowadays as, not only are the fine threads unavailable to the modern lacemaker, but certain of the techniques seem to be lost for ever. Therefore, it is of the utmost importance that we design laces suitable for modern-day equipment and more typical of our present life style.

Very few ladies, for example, could now afford to employ a maid solely to look after their laces; the maid's only tasks being to detach the laces from garments for laundering, mending them when necessary and then replacing them. Clothing must be able to be put straight into the washing machine and drip-dried, because lack of time is the bugbear of the modern housewife and mother who often also goes out to work. Fashion and convenience, then, decree that we use lace trimmings on our clothes only spasmodically, according to the whims of designers and clothing manufacturers, but lace-trimmed household linens are still as popular as ever and there are other uses to which lace can be put. The idea of lace pictures, paperweights, bookmarks, lampshades and Christmas decorations is recent, as are the three-dimensional models designed of late. Making lace in different colours using various textures is worth exploring, too. The white, ecru and black threads that have always been available have now been supplemented with those of a wealth of colour and thickness. When working the trunk of a tree into a design, for example, it is now possible to obtain the texture and colour of the bark in addition to the basic outline.

Traditional materials are still essential to the lacemaker today, however. The natural fibres of silk, linen, cotton and wool all hold their shapes when pins are removed, but just try working with nylon or Terylene thread and the results are most disappointing.

One unsuspecting lacemaker when only a beginner, spent the whole of her Christmas holiday making an edging in a Bedfordshire pattern with a ninepin head-side for a favourite traycloth. She used Terylene sewing thread. Imagine her horror when the whole thing collapsed, rolling itself up into a ball, as the pins were taken out! Nearly in tears, she arrived for her next lesson and sought advice. Eventually, she managed to salvage the lace by re-pinning the whole edging back on her pillow and spray-starching the whole thing. She now uses it on her dressing table under a sheet of plate glass. It can never be laundered for fear that it will lose its shape again. So be warned!

Changing techniques

Just because something has always been done in a certain fashion, does not mean that this is necessarily the best way of doing it. On the other hand, change for the sake of itself is a bad thing, and techniques in lacemaking should only be altered if materials demand it or if the new method improves the look of the finished lace. Needless to say, any change that makes life easier for the lacemaker must be beneficial.

One instance of this is that nowadays there is not always a necessity to prick patterns onto pricking card. Once, there was no other way of producing a satisfactory firm base for the pins. With the advent of fine-grain card and polythene sheeting, if a pattern is only to be worked once or twice, there is no need to perform this laborious task. Providing that the pillow is rock hard and the card of fine grain, the photostat copy produced from the patterns in this book need not be reproduced on pricking card. Indeed, their accuracy could be impaired by poor or careless pricking. Two types of card that are suitable for this purpose are cereal packets and the stiff card found in packs of new tights or shirts.

If a lacemaker has difficulty in seeing white threads when working on a white pattern, there are several alternatives open to her. One of them is to colour over the design with a yellow or pale green felt-tip pen. The colour does not run once it is dry and, therefore, the thread is not discoloured. Another idea is to purchase some self-adhesive film that has a faint blue or green tinge and to stick this over the pattern. When using coloured or black threads, however, it can be positively beneficial to be working on a white pattern.

Bobbin lacemaking is one of the most versatile crafts there is. A single design can be worked more than once, using a variety of thicknesses of threads and a change of distance between the pinholes, thus giving a completely different effect and use for the finished lace. Even the stitches can be varied within a laid-down design to alter the look of the pattern. It is remarkable that the same basic stitch can be used with such a large number of pin arrangements to achieve the traditional designs so typical of various countries, or even regions within a country.

Every lacemaker has a 'blind spot' or a stitch that she really dislikes working. Maybe it is a braid with picots, or half-stitch blocks, or even the straight edge. When designing, it is usually possible to avoid the least favourite stitch and to substitute another. It can be seen from the patterns in this book that the designer prefers to avoid working tallies unless absolutely necessary.

Finally, it is to be hoped that the lacemaker working these designs will be inspired to create something of her own, and thus the 1980s and 1990s could become a time when our craft blossomed out just as it did in centuries past.

2 Equipment

Pillows

A lacemaker's pillow is undoubtedly the most important part of her equipment and it is also the most individual. Recently, at an Adult Education Centre, a prospective lacemaker enrolled after the commencement of term. She asked the Principal what equipment she would need to bring to her first class. He, in his innocence, told her that the students needed a cushion but any other equipment was obtained from the tutor. She still recalls the horror she felt when she entered the classroom, clutching a large feather cushion, and saw the neat, hard pillows in use by her fellow students.

Every lacemaker has her own favourite pillow, preferring it to all others for reasons of shape, perhaps, or weight, or even for sentimental reasons. If a group of people are given identical instructions for making a pillow, rarely will any two be identical as each pillow bears its maker's imprint. The ready-made pillows available for purchase by the lacemaker to-day can never replace her own hand-made one, but they do serve a great need, especially for those unable to construct their own for one reason or another.

To make the lace in this book, two different types of pillow are required. A flat, round pillow is used for the majority of the patterns, but a bolster pillow is invaluable for others. The continental type of pillow with a small roller inserted may prove difficult to use as an alternative to a bolster pillow due to the width of the patterns concerned.

The flat pillow

The 51 cm (20 in) diameter flat pillow described below is a little larger than the traditional 41–46 cm (16–18 in) one, but it has the advantage of permitting a reasonably large piece of lace to be made without the necessity of moving the lace up the pillow, always a tedious and laborious task. An extra benefit is that the large number of bobbins needed for some of the fillings can be disposed of in a more convenient fashion without the threads becoming tangled.

To make this pillow, the following materials are needed.

Item 1 A circular piece of 3-ply wood, about 51 cm (20 in) in diameter.

Item 2 A circular piece of finely woven material, 5 cm (2 in) larger than the plywood. Old sheeting is ideal for this.

Item 3 A circular piece of plain, dark blue cotton material 8 cm (3 in) larger than the plywood.

Item 4 Narrow tape, about the length of the circumference of the wood.

Item 5 Sawdust, animal bedding, wood wool, straw or similar material for filling.

Item 6 'UHU' glue or a similar type.

Item 7 A circular piece of material of the same type as for Item 2, but 2·5 cm (1 in) smaller than the plywood.

Cut a hole in the centre of the plywood large enough to put a hand in. (Keep this centre piece and do not smooth the edges of the hole.) Place Item 2 over the base and stick the edge of the material firmly to the reverse side only. Fill the space between the material and plywood with the sawdust etc. through the central hole, making sure that the filling reaches the very edge. Do not make this too domed or it will prove difficult to produce lace that will lie flat and to keep the bobbins evenly in position. To prevent the pillow from 'doming' whilst filling it, place it upside-down on the floor and rotate it continually with one hand whilst pushing the filling in with the other hand, making sure that the edge of the pillow is well padded.

Carry on filling until the pillow is rock hard and it is impossible to get any more in. There should be a small pile of filling material protruding from the hole. Replace the centre plywood plug and secure with masking tape or other adhesive tape.

Now take the piece of material which is smaller than the plywood (Item 7) and stick it firmly over the base of the pillow with glue. Make a narrow hem round the edge of the dark blue material. Thread the tape through this hem and place the material over the pillow, drawing the tape up tightly on the reverse side. This makes a removable cover for the pillow. Tuck in the loose ends of the tape. The pillow is now ready for use.

The bolster pillow

To make a bolster pillow, the materials that are required are as follows.

Figure 1 A flat pillow in use: the larger diameter pillow allows plenty of space for the bobbins not in use to be disposed of evenly

Item 1 A piece of strong, finely woven material 76·5 × 46 cm (30 × 18 in). White or coloured sheeting is ideal.

Item 2 A piece of dark blue cotton material the same size as Item 1.

Item 3 4 metres (4 yards) narrow cotton tape.

Item 4 Straw, hay, sawdust, wood wool or any combination of these for filling.

Item 5 Two small discs of cardboard about 15 cm (6 in) in diameter.

Using Item 1, join the short sides together to make a tube of material. Now make a narrow hem on each of the ends of this tube and thread a quarter of the narrow tape through each hem. Turn inside-out and draw up one end tightly. Place one of the cardboard discs over the small hole that is left, and start to fill the pillow from the other end. A hammer will probably be needed to bang the filling down in order to obtain sufficient firmness. Make sure that the pillow is not lumpy when finished.

If straw or hay is used, it will be necessary to cut it into small lengths before filling the pillow. It is amazing how much material really goes into one of these pillows. Inevitably, with straw or hay, small gaps are still left and, therefore, it can be helpful to mix in some sawdust or wood chippings with the straw to ensure a really firm finish. If sawdust is used on its own, the finished weight of the pillow will be considerable. To assist in obtaining a smooth surface, roll the pillow about, using it like a rolling pin, with a firm movement.

When the pillow appears over-full, draw up the second end tightly, placing the other cardboard disc just inside the pillow under the hole that is left. Tuck in the ends of the tape.

Make a cover using the dark blue material in a similar fashion and slip it over the pillow. However much filling is used when making this type of pillow, it is nearly always found that more filling is needed after it has been used a little. It is a very simple task to open up one end and add more filling.

The cover for the lace pillow has always been traditionally of dark blue cotton or linen material. Back in the sixteenth century, dark blue dye was more readily available than others and linen or cotton the only fabric to hand. It is not necessary to use a dark blue fabric nowadays, although many lacemakers prefer to keep to tradition. Any dark colour is just as acceptable, be it brown, green, purple or plum colour. What is essential, however, is that the material has no pattern, as this can be a distraction for the user, nor must it be fluffy or have any loosely woven threads in which the spangles and bobbins could become entangled.

Cover cloths

These can be made in the traditional manner by using the same material as the pillow cover, but large man-size handkerchiefs or napkins would serve the purpose equally well.

When working braid laces, the bobbins frequently lie over the work already done and, when using a cover cloth over the pins, the pinheads can protrude through the material even when they are pushed fully into the pillow. For this sort of work it is better to use a sheet of thick, clear plastic over the pillow rather than the traditional cover cloth. There is an added bonus in doing this, in that the work already completed can be seen through the plastic. The plastic sheet should be about the same size as the pillow, with a hole in the centre to leave a space clear for the work in hand. The bobbins then run smoothly over the work. To measure the size of the hole needed, use a teacup or the base of a Coke can (or similar) and draw round this to give an even circle. Then cut it out with scissors, making sure not to leave any uneven or jagged parts of the edge.

Bobbins

The variety of bobbins now available would amaze the lacemaker of 100 years ago. Not only are there so many different size variations, but the materials of which they are made are so diverse. Although bobbins are often still made of wood, bone and ivory, plastic bobbins are now common as are ones made of brass, silver, anodised metal, glass and even chopsticks and 4-inch nails.

It has been discovered that the marrowbones used by bobbin makers over the centuries have become much smaller during the twentieth century. Apparently, this is due to the need for more economy in the breeding of cattle to produce a greater quantity of flesh and less bone. Hence, it is only possible to obtain perhaps two or three bobbins from one bone instead of the six or seven once produced.

The bobbin maker of the 1980s is certainly proving very versatile and every bit as dextrous as his predecessors. If quantity rather than quality is the main consideration for the lacemaker, a cheap plastic bobbin will do the same work as an expensive ivory or antique one. It does not matter about mixing bobbins of different materials on the pillow either, but it is best to have bobbins of a like size and weight working together. It is also better to use larger bobbins for thicker threads and to keep the smaller ones for the finer threads.

Spangles

It has always been the tradition for certain of our English bobbins to be weighted with glass beads or spangles, rather than to use the shape of the bobbin itself to act as its own weight. The purpose of these beads is really to ensure that a light-weight, slim bobbin provides sufficient weight at the end of the thread being used to give a good tension to the work and to hold the thread in place on the pillow. In reality, they also produce a very pleasing decorative appearance to the pillow whilst in use and they help prevent the bobbins from rolling about too much.

Tradition and superstition have always required that a pillow has a bobbin in use with a coin on it to ensure good fortune, and a button on another bobbin as an extra good luck token for the lacemaker and her family. It is not essential to abide by this, though, and many bobbins are seen nowadays with polished stones or charms and medallions acting as weights. Ceramic beads are also excellent, but the cheap, plastic, mass-produced ones are of no use whatsoever as they weigh virtually nothing.

Most lace suppliers have very good stocks of beautiful but rather pricey beads. Jumble sales can often be a cheap source of supply as can Granny's jewellery box, but do not dismantle a string of pearls to use as spangles only to discover too late that they are the genuine article and not imitation!

When attaching the beads to the bobbins, it is best to use a good quality brass wire and to ensure that the sharp cut ends are neatly tucked in. Many a spangle has been lost by using a cotton thread or too thin a wire for this purpose. The wire ends may catch in the cover cloth or cause snags in the thread of the lace if they are not neatly finished.

Figure 2 European bobbins: the amount of wood in the bobbins gives sufficient weight

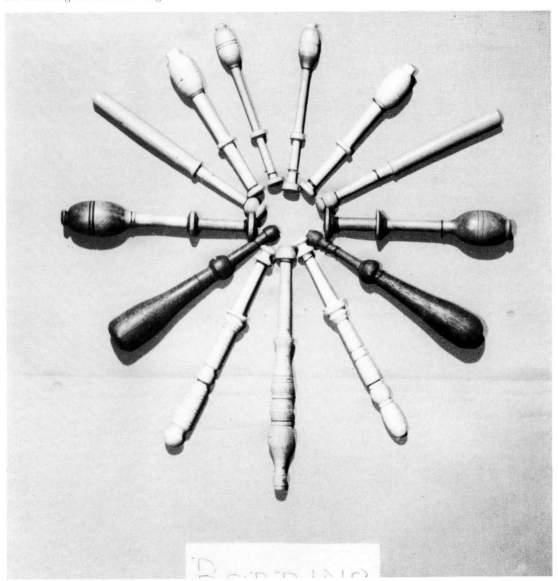

Pins

It is essential to use brass pins either of the yellow or the white variety. An old toffee tin full of brass pins was discovered recently, together with other lace equipment. It had been in a damp attic for nearly 40 years and yet those pins, although very badly discoloured, were not rusty. They were tested, in use with some new pins of the same weight and size. They proved to leave no mark on the finished lace and have since regained some of their original colour through continual use.

Different sizes of pins are used for varying thicknesses of thread, the criterion being that the thicker the thread, the stronger the pin needed. Another factor which determines the size of pin required for a particular pattern, is the distance between the pinholes in the design. If the pins are too thick, the holes formed by them will cause the lace to be incorrect in the final appearance.

Berry pins are a useful accessory as they have more strength than brass pins. They are useful as pivot pins or on the edge of a thick-thread pattern. Remember, though, that they are not made of brass and should not be left in damp conditions,

Figure 3 English bobbins: beads are used for weight on slim bobbins

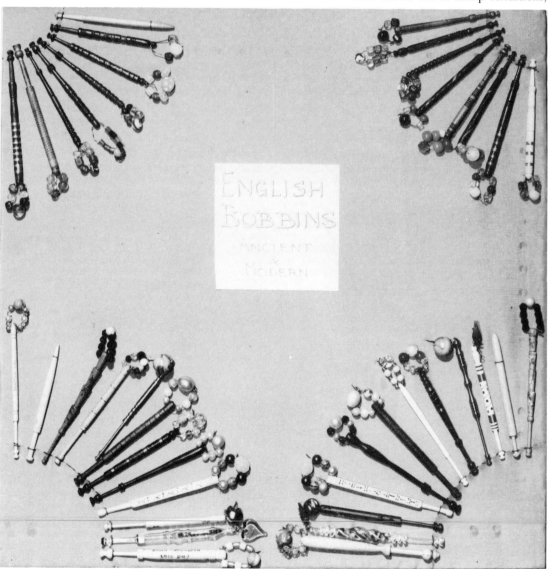

especially when in use on the pillow. No lacemaker wishes to find the edge of her work marked by unsightly rust patches left by non-brass pins.

Pincushions

It has always been traditional for a lacemaker to have a pincushion attached to her pillow in order to keep the pins that are in use at a convenient distance from her work. This does not have to be hard like the pillow, but it is very useful to fill it with emery granules. These serve to keep the pins sharp and also clear of dulling film. It is helpful to have several small pincushions, using each one for different sized pins to avoid mixing them up.

When working tape lace, however, a pincushion can sometimes be a positive nuisance, because it has to be continually moved around the pillow in order to be out of the way of the bobbins being worked. In this instance, it is better to have the pins needed in a small wooden pot or tin. Provided that the pillow is kept horizontal, this

Figure 4 Lacemaking equipment: thread, scissors, pincushion, berry pins, bobbin winder, bobbin hanger, chest of drawers with bobbins

does not slide off and it is easier to move around.

Thread

Ideally, one should use the best quality thread available. It seems a pity that a lacemaker should spend so much time on producing her lace only to find the finished product is inferior due to poor thread. Linen holds its shape far better than cotton although, unfortunately, it is not possible to purchase it in the variety of colours sometimes required.

It is better to avoid any thread which is not specifically spun for lacemaking as the twist is not necessarily correct. If, of course, it is possible to discover a thread which has the correct twist, it is perfectly permissible to use it, but work a small

15

sample first before commencing the actual piece of lace.

Silk thread makes excellent lace but, if the lacemaker's hands or bobbins have any rough patches, it is liable to snag. There is also a slight problem with fraying ends when tying knots and finishing the lace. Wool is good, too, but it is a bit 'springy' and the threads must be continually pulled firmly into place. The other problem with wool is the fact that it is so thick that the length of thread able to be wound on the bobbin at one time is shorter than with finer threads. There are, therefore, inevitably more joins in the finished work.

Scissors

A really sharp pair of embroidery scissors with fine points is essential. Trying to cut threads with blunt scissors causes the thread to be pulled rather than cleanly cut and this is untidy. Similarly, blunt-ended scissors cannot always reach between the pins to cut threads short enough and this leaves ragged ends.

Bobbin winders

These are not strictly necessary as many patterns do not require a very long length of thread on the bobbins. When working fillings, especially for braid patterns, a length of thread long enough to wind 12–24 times round a bobbin is frequently sufficient.

It is, however, very useful to have one of these machines and there are a number of excellent ready-made ones on the market, but they are rather costly. It is possible to make a 'Heath Robinson' bobbin winder, based on the commercial ones, out of scraps of wood and elastic bands and these are usually just as effective.

Pillow stands

Once again, not a strictly essential part of a modern lacemaker's equipment but an added luxury. The variety of stands for the lacemaker today is endless. As well as the traditional shapes developed in different parts of the country, there are modern designs which are equally practical.

The type of stand used really depends on the shape of the pillow. The bow-shaped traditional one, or 'pillow horse' as it was called, is the best stand for a bolster pillow, but a satisfactory table-

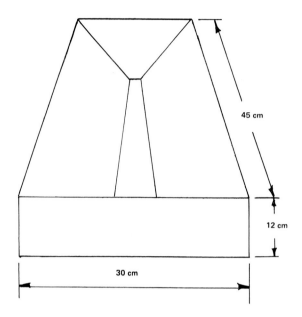

Diagram 1 Table-top pillow stand

45 cm

12 cm

30 cm

top version can be made from a shallow box slightly larger than the pillow. Sloping sides are formed to fit the pillow, and a thick sheet of foam is glued to the inside of the finished box which can be covered on the outside with sticky-backed plastic to enhance its appearance and to give a little more strength. Diagram 1 shows the approximate dimensions needed for one of these. The foam gives a firm base on which to rest the pillow and prevents it from slipping round when in use.

When choosing a stand for a flat pillow, versatility should be the main criterion. Choose a stand that has the ability to tilt to any required angle, and which will be adaptable for any height of chair the worker may use. It must also be possible to attach the pillow firmly to the stand. There is nothing worse than working a pattern with many pairs of bobbins on the pillow, and, on returning to the work after a short period of absence, finding that the pillow has been upset and all the bobbins disarrayed.

Securing bobbins to a pillow for transportation

When a pillow is transported from one place to another, the bobbins inevitably roll about and become displaced. In order to prevent this happening a wide piece of elastic or tape can be pinned over them ensuring that enough pins are used to separate the bobbins into pairs or small groups.

Alternatively, a second pillow cover, can be made, identical to the one made for the pillow in use. Instead of threading the hem with tape, use narrow elastic. This cover can then be fitted snugly over the pillow, bobbins, pins and all, and will keep the bobbins in place.

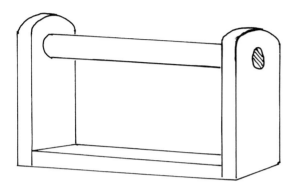

Diagram 2 Bobbin hanger

Bobbin hangers

When a number of pairs of bobbins need to be prepared in one session, there is always the problem of how to keep them from becoming tangled up with one another. Of course, they can be set out in pairs on a table or laid over the arm of an armchair, but if this is not possible, it is very useful to have a small rail on which to hang the bobbins.

These can be bought at reasonable cost or made at home from a length of old broom handle covered in sticky-backed felt fabric. This is slotted into a stand as shown in diagram 2. The height of the rail from the base should be as long as a bobbin plus spangles, and the length can be made to suit the individual requirements of the lacemaker, but preferrably not longer than 30 cm (12 in).

Bobbin cases

It is always a problem to know how to store bobbins when they are not in use to prevent them being lost or broken. A 2- or 4-litre ice cream carton or a similar plastic box is ideal for the beginner, but, sooner or later, something better is required. There are some beautiful wooden bobbin boxes and small chest of drawers sets for those with space for them but many lacemakers make a neat carrying case for their bobbins out of a length of strong material.

Take a piece of material approximately 50 cm (20 in) long, and fold the sides towards the centre. In effect, the width should be four times the length of a bobbin plus twice the length of the spangles. Leave sufficient space in the centre for two sets of spangles. Hem the turned-in edges and sew down the folded sides to make pockets for the bobbins. Attach two lengths of narrow tape to one end. When the bobbins are all in place, the case can be folded in half lengthwise and rolled up. The tapes are used to tie the bundle securely.

Diagram 3 Bobbin case

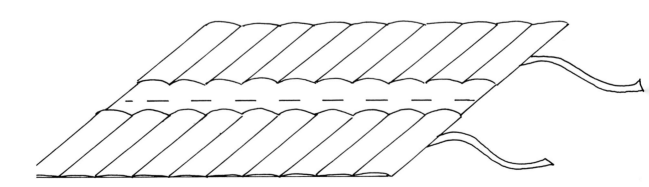

Carrying cases

Transporting pillows can often prove difficult. Some lacemakers tie up their pillows in a large piece of material, making a knot at the centre, and carry them flat. Others manage to find a very large plastic carrier bag. But it is not difficult to make a more permanent carrying case using strong cotton or canvas material and two sturdy zip fasteners.

Cut two circles of material a little larger than the pillow and one strip of the same material about 10 cm (4 in) wide, long enough to reach right round the circumference of these circles. The two zips each need to be at least one-quarter of the circumference of the pillow. First, attach the zips to the long strip of material. Cut the strip in half lengthwise from each of the ends as long as the zip fasteners. This means that the cuts will reach one-quarter of the way round from each end. Now the zips can be firmly sewn with the open ends at either end of the strip of material. Sew one edge of this long strip to the edge of one of the circular pieces of material, putting the right sides together. Now repeat this with the other edge and the second circle of material. Open the zips and turn to the right side. Attach two strong handles which can either be bought or made out of rope covered with the same material. One handle is sewn to each side (see diagram 4), so that the point where the zip fasteners meet is central at the top. The pillow will slide comfortably into the case when both zips are fully open.

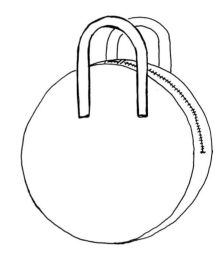

Diagram 4 Carrying case

3 Stitches used in lacemaking

It is presumed that the lacemaker wishing to make these patterns has already a knowledge of the basic techniques and, therefore, the section of stitches is kept to a minimum. It is intended to serve as a reminder rather than as an instruction.

Basic stitch

This is worked in three movements (see diagram 5).

1 Pass bobbin 2 over bobbin 3.
2 Pass bobbin 2 over bobbin 1, and bobbin 4 over bobbin 3.
3 Pass bobbin 2 over bobbin 3.

It is not necessary to remember where each numbered bobbin has travelled as the bobbins are renumbered after each movement.

Half stitch

This is worked by using the first two movements in the basic, or whole-stitch sequence only.

Twists

A twist is made by passing the right-hand bobbin of a pair over the left-hand bobbin. If more than one twist is indicated on a pattern, repeat this movement as necessary. A twist is indicated on a pattern by a short sloping line across the line of direction of the threads. The number of twists is shown by the number of sloping lines.

Straight edges

Normal foot braid

Work up to the outside passive pair. Twist the workers once and work a whole stitch with the

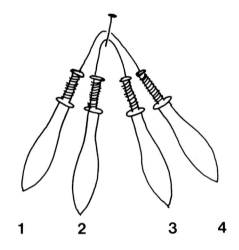

1 **2** **3** **4**

one whole stitch

one half stitch

Diagram 5 The basic stitch

outside passive pair. Now twist the workers three times and the outside passives once. Put a pin inside both of these pairs. Leave the worker to one side and use the outside passive pair as workers until this edge is reached again, when this movement is repeated. Do *not* work another whole stitch on the edge to enclose the pin. In diagram 6 each pair of bobbins is represented by a single line.

Whole-stitch braids

This straight edge is worked similarly to the normal foot braid and the workers are still changed at the end of each row. But the workers are only twisted once after working through the outside pair of passives at the changeover. The passives are not twisted at all, neither are the workers twisted before working the last pair of passives. This keeps the edge firm and straight, but does not allow too large a gap between the passives and the edge.

Plaits

A plait is worked by firstly completing one whole stitch and thereafter working movements two and three of the whole-stitch sequence consecutively, until the plait is long enough. Always end with 2 over 3.

When plaits need to be crossed, a simple technique called a 'windmill' or 'lazy join' is employed. Using each pair of bobbins as if it is a single bobbin, work a half stitch with the four pairs. Now put in the pin and work 2 over 3 to complete a whole stitch. The plaits are now ready to be continued, commencing each with a whole stitch. If the plaits are not merely crossed, but one of them is used for the side of a pattern, it is better to work a whole stitch before and after the pin. Remember, though, not to twist the bobbins as this is worked.

Picots

These can be worked at the side of a plait or at the edge of a piece of lace. When reaching the pin at which a picot is to be worked, take bobbin 1 (see diagram 8) which is the left-hand bobbin for a left-hand picot. Lay a pin on the thread and twist the thread up and over the pin. Now, still holding the bobbin on which the thread has been twisted round the pin, put the pin in. Tighten the thread and pass it under the next bobbin to the right (2 over 1). The plait can now be continued starting

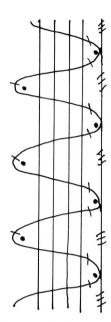

Diagram 6 Putting a straight edge on a braid

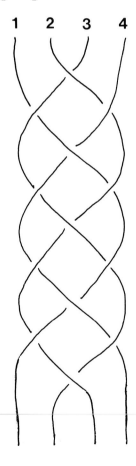

Diagram 7 A plait

20

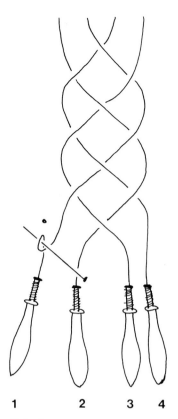

1 **2** **3** **4**

Diagram 8 A picot

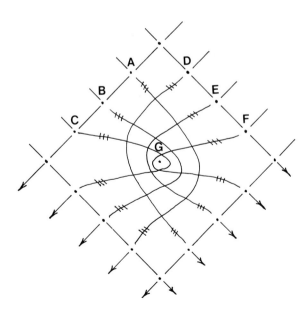

Diagram 9 Working a spider

with a complete whole stitch or the whole-stitch block at the edge of the lace may be worked, whatever the case may be.

If the picot is to be worked at the right-hand side of the plait, use bobbin 4 instead of 1 and after tightening the thread round the inserted pin, twist 4 over 3. This is only to work a single picot. Double picots are not dealt with in this book.

There are several other ways of working picots which are equally effective. The only proviso when using the method shown here is that the plait must be worked tightly and right up to the pinhole. Also, after working the picot, in order that it will not become loose, continue working the plait in the same direction as before, even if it is marked as working in another direction on the pattern. After about four repeats of the stitch, still ensuring that the bobbin that passed round the pin to form the picot is kept tightly held, the plait can be gently turned in the correct direction and the picot should not become slack.

Spiders

These can be worked with any number of pairs of legs at either side providing that there are the same number of legs on each side. These instructions are given for a small spider of three legs each side and the diagram shows each pair of bobbins as a single line. The smallest spider has two legs on either side.

1 Twist each pair three times. Take the pair from A and work whole stitches through the pairs from D, E and F.

2 Take the pair from B and work whole stitches through the pairs from D, E and F.

3 Take the pair from C and work whole stitches through the same three pairs.

4 Now put in the pin at G with all threads above the pin.

5 Take the third pair from the right and work whole stitches through the three pairs to the left.

6 Take the second pair from the right and work whole stitches through the next three pairs to the left.

7 Take the right-hand pair and work whole stitches through the next three pairs to the left.

8 Pull the threads tight and twist all pairs three times.

The threads are now ready to join the next section of work. When working spiders with more

21

than four legs each side, ensure that the body is evenly shaped round the centre pin. To do this, attach the legs on alternate sides when completing the spider.

Tallies

These are worked with two pairs of bobbins. Work a whole stitch first with these two pairs after putting the pin in to make a firm start. Now lengthen the thread of bobbin 3. This is used to weave round the other threads to form a solid block which is shaped by moving the two outside passives further apart and then nearer to one another.

Commence the weaving by passing the weaver under bobbin 4; round and back over 4; under bobbin 2; over bobbin 1; and round back under 1; over 2, and so on. The three passives can either be held in the hand or laid flat on the pillow. Every lacemaker has to discover for herself the most convenient way. It is very important not to release the tension on the weaver or the tally will probably pull out of shape. Likewise, care must be taken to ensure that the sides are smooth or the finished tally could look like a holly leaf!

After each line of weaving, ensure that the threads are firmly in position. When the tally reaches the end, for a leaf shape, the four threads should be close together again and the weaver is back in its original position of 3. If the tally is to be attached to the rest of the work very soon, it is sufficient to twist 2 over 1 and 4 over 3 and then to lay the weaver to the back of the work in order to keep the tension on it. If the tally is not to be used for some time, it is best to tie the weaver round the other three threads in the style of working a

sewing. If the tally looks neat when completed and attached to the rest of the lace then that method is correct for that particular lacemaker.

Ten stick

This is a stitch normally used only in Honiton lace but it can be particularly useful in 'free' lace designs when a tendril or similar shape is required. It is worked using only one line of pinholes. The minimum number of pairs of bobbins that are needed is three, but more are used if the tendril is to be thicker.

Always commence at the end that is not attached to the stem. Hang the bobbins on a pin at that point. Work a whole stitch with the two pairs on the outer side of the curve and twist both pairs once. **Work the inner of these two pairs through the rest of the threads in whole stitch and twist once at the end. Do not use a pin at this point but take the last pair worked through and work back to the outside in whole stitch. Twist both pairs once and put a pin inside these as for a straight edge. Repeat from ** until the required length is reached. The diagram shows the commencement of a ten-stick tendril using four pairs of bobbins.

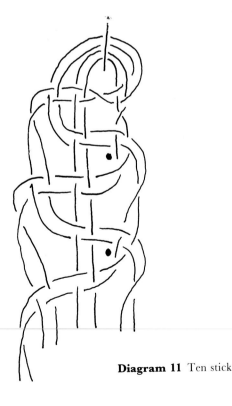

Diagram 10 A tally

Diagram 11 Ten stick

22

4 Techniques

1 Commencing a plain braid

Hang two pairs of bobbins on a pin at A and the rest on pins evenly distributed along a line. One of the pairs at A is the worker. Work whole stitch through every passive pair until only one pair remains unworked. Twist the workers twice. Pass them behind pin B, round the outside of the work, and now work a whole stitch with the passive pair hanging on pin B. This is the first whole stitch of the second line of work.

Continue the braid normally, twisting the workers once or twice at the edge as the pattern demands. This method of commencing a braid ensures that the join on completion is very neat and almost undetectable on the right side of the work.

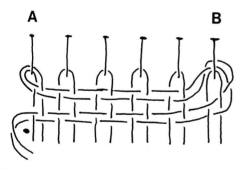

Diagram 12 Commencing a plain braid

2 Commencing a Bruges flower/braid

Hang pairs of bobbins on pins as directed in the pattern. Starting at pin A which has two pairs of bobbins hanging on it, work a whole stitch and twist both pairs. Now work in whole stitch through the rest of the passives except the last. Twist the workers twice and pass behind pin B, round the outside of the work, and work a whole stitch with the pair hanging on pin B. Twist both pairs once.

The first petal of the Bruges flower is worked in whole stitch, twisting the workers once before working the outside passive pairs; twice outside the pin and twisting both pairs once after enclosing the pin with a whole stitch. The braid in Bruges flower work is always worked in this fashion unless it is a

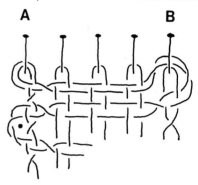

Diagram 13 Commencing a Bruges flower/braid

half-stitch braid. Then the outside passives are worked in whole stitch and both pairs twisted. Alternate petals in the flowers are also worked in this fashion.

3 Commencing by hanging threads on a single pin

When commencing a piece of work from a single pin, never hang more than four pairs of bobbins on the pin. Twist the outside pair three times and work one of these pairs in the direction of the next pin to be worked.

Always hang the threads round the pin as shown in diagram 14 (a) and never as in diagram 14 (b), otherwise when the pin is removed on completion of the lace, there will be four separate loops. This makes the finished work untidy and, if a sewing is necessary into this point, it is almost impossible to do neatly.

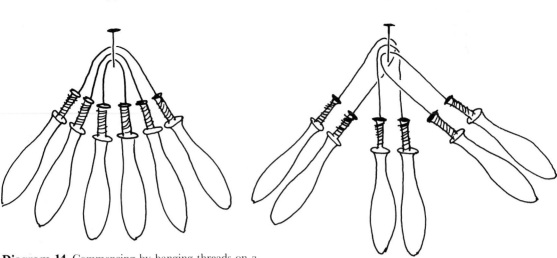

A   **B**

Diagram 14 Commencing by hanging threads on a single pin (a) (b)

4 Commencing Torchon lace

When commencing a length of Torchon lace which is to be joined as a complete unit (for example: an edging or a square mat), always commence at one corner on the diagonal line of pins. Hang the bobbins on pins at the places where they will eventually finish. Work the first block or line of pins and then take out the pins on which the threads were originally hung. Ease the loops so formed by wriggling the bobbins until the loops disappear into the lace just worked.

There is now a neat line of threads in preparation for the continuation of the lace. Make sure that the first complete pattern repeat, at least, is left with pins not removed, to facilitate the finishing.

5 Bruges scrolls

Put a thicker pin than used for the rest of the work at point A. Hang four pairs of bobbins on this pin as shown in diagram 14 (a), with the threads lying in the direction of the arrow. Twist the outside pair five times. Now take the right-hand pair and work out to pin B, twisting the workers before the last whole stitch and twice after it. Now put a pin at B; work a whole stitch to enclose this pin; and twist both pairs.

The aim is now to increase the number of pairs of bobbins in the work until the optimum number is reached. Add one pair per row or each alternate row, whichever keeps the block of whole stitch flat and firm. This is described in Technique 8 (p. 25). Pin A is worked as a pivot pin (see Technique 21, p. 29) keeping the innermost pair – the unworked

passives—twisted three times until pin C has been worked. Now work towards pin D. Take out the pivot pin A and, with the innermost pair, do a sewing into the first row of work, pushing aside all the threads except the bottom ones. Pull this pair up neatly and the scroll should be flat. The pile of threads that were building up the pivot pin have dispersed evenly. Twist the pair that has just worked the sewing, and use it as the outside twisted passive pair for the ensuing braid.

When finishing a braid in a Bruges scroll, the method is to work the above instructions in reverse. Omitting the sewings at pin D, work the

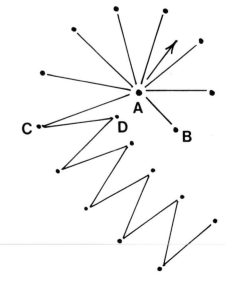

Diagram 15 A Bruges scroll

24

braid using the pivot pin and losing pairs gradually as for Technique 12 (p. 27). By the time the last outside pin (pin B) has been worked, there should only be three pairs of passives and a worker pair left. Now work through the passives, round the pivot pin, and back out, leaving the workers to the side. Remove the pivot pin and work a sewing into the first stitch that was round it (at the base of the pile of threads) with the unworked passive pair. Each of the other passive pairs must now be sewn into the same hole, followed finally by the workers. Tie each pair and cut the ends short.

6 Commencing corners

This is a neat and efficient method of commencing a piece of lace whose edges are to be joined to another like piece as a seam, using back stitch or flat stitch. Hang two pairs of bobbins on pins at A, B and D. With the left-hand pair from A, work in whole stitch through the other pair from A and both pairs from D. With the right-hand pair from B, work in whole stitch through the same three pairs. With the left-hand pair from B, work in whole stitch through the same three pairs, but put a pin at E between the last passives and the worker. At pin E, an extra pair must be added as in Technique 9 (p. 26) for the main ground. Now enclose the pin with the two pairs from B and D and use these respectively as the workers for the braids in directions M and N.

7 Turning corners

After the workers have travelled through the passives on the top braid, they become the inside passive pair of the side braid. Take the outside passive pair from the top braid. Put in a pin at B with these passives (twisted twice), passing round the outside of this pin. Now work them in whole stitch through the inside passives from the top braid and put them beside the pair that worked round pin A.

Take the inside passives from the top braid. Put in a pin at C and pass these (twisted twice) round the outside of this pin. The pillow can now be turned round through 90 degrees (a right angle) and this pair will be used as the workers for the outside braid down the side of the work.

8 Adding in new threads for whole-stitch blocks

When the braid or block of whole stitch widens and the number of passives is not sufficient to give a close-knit appearance to the work, more passives must be added. The following method has proved very satisfactory both in the look of the finished lace and in the ease of working.

Work across the lace until one pair of passives is left unworked. Hang a new pair of bobbins on a pin outside the work being done. Lay the threads between the unworked pair thus separating the

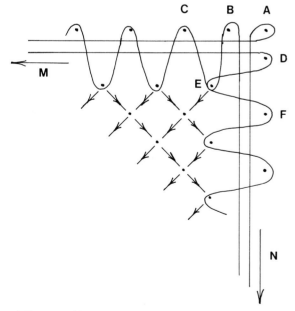

Diagram 16 Commencing corners

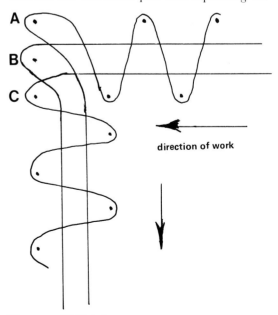

Diagram 17 Turning corners

pairs (see diagram 18). Never put one of the threads of the new pair to the outside of a block of whole stitch although they may be added at any part of the body of the work providing they lie with one of the passives already incorporated between them.

Now work in whole stitch across both of these pairs and continue as normal. After three or four rows of work using the new pair, their pin can be removed and the threads eased down neatly into place.

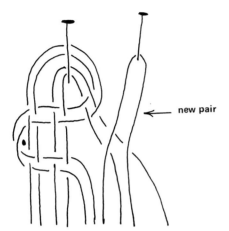

Diagram 18 Adding in new pairs for whole-stitch blocks

9 Hanging in new threads for fillings whilst working the outside braid

In order to add threads for the centre of the lace simultaneously to working the outside braid, a simple technique can be used. Work across the braid until the pin is reached at which the pair is to be added. Now take the new pair and lay it on the pillow between the passives of the braid and the workers (diagram 19a). Work a whole stitch with this new pair and the workers and put them to the side where they are to be used (diagram 19b). Now put the pin in between the workers and the passives of the braid and continue with the braid. The new pair is now ready for working the main body of the lace.

10 Hanging in a new pair (fillings)

When working with coloured or thicker threads, the traditional way of joining in a new pair of bobbins with a complete sewing can appear bulky or untidy. The following method is just as effective and much neater. Wind one bobbin with thread and leave an end about 45 cm (18 in) long, take out the pin at the point where the threads are to be added. Insert the crochet hook and pull the thread on the bobbin right through the loop made by the threads already round the pinhole. Now replace the pin and wind the length of thread pulled through onto another bobbin to make a pair hanging in that place.

Normally fillings do not take very much thread although a great number of bobbins are used, so it is unnecessary to wind the bobbins fully.

Diagram 19 Hanging in new pairs

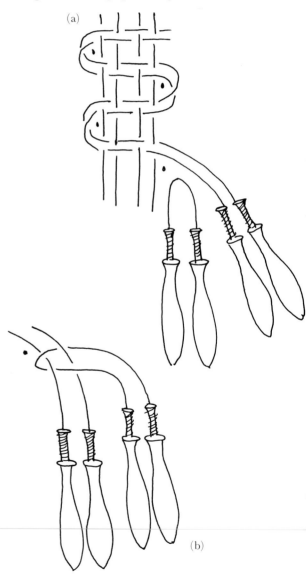

11 Adding or removing pairs from half-stitch blocks

The technique for these procedures is almost identical as for whole-stitch blocks with the exception that they are *always* added or removed next to the edge. The whole-stitch pair at the edge is ignored, and the first and third threads in from there are discarded or added as the case may be. Alternatively, the inside thread from the whole-stitch edge pair may be used with the second thread in from there.

It is advisable to tie the discarded threads before cutting them as a half-stitch block does not hold the threads as firmly as a whole-stitch block.

12 Losing threads (whole-stitch blocks)

When a block of whole-stitch work narrows and less threads are indicated, the best way to lose them is as follows. As for the technique of adding more pairs to whole-stitch blocks, pairs are never taken from the outside threads nor are adjacent ones ever discarded. The former means an untidy edge and, perhaps, the threads becoming unwoven in time, and the latter forms a hole in the fabric. Neither must the threads be taken out until the passives are really closely packed together.

When absolutely sure that a pair must be discarded, before commencing a row of whole stitch, take the second and fourth passives from the outside and lay them to the back of the work, then continue as normal. The next pair to be lost should be at the other edge in order that the discarded threads have an even distribution over the width of the work. When that section of lace has been completed, these discarded threads can be cut close to the work in the knowledge that they will not become dislodged due to the closeness of the remaining passives.

13 Losing threads (fillings)

When working a filling, there are frequent places where the threads are discarded, either to rejoin shortly or to be finished completely.

If they are to be rejoined immediately, work a sewing into the pin at the point where they leave the filling (see Technique 19, p. 28); replace the pin. They will now be ready to rejoin the work, instead of hanging in a new pair, or they can be carried down the outside braid at the side of the filling to rejoin at the next pin.

If they are not to be worked again, after working the sewing and replacing the pin, tie them twice, making sure that the knot is over the braid to the side of the filling. Do not cut the threads until some more of the work has been completed because it has been known for knots to become undone whilst a sewing is being worked at the following pin-hole.

14 Losing threads through the outside braid

This technique is used when working pieces of lace which are to be joined together with a seam. The threads are discarded as the lace grows narrower or the end of the lace is worked. Work until the point where the threads are to be removed is reached. Before working the edge braid workers back to the outside, work the pair to be discarded through the edge passives in whole stitch and leave to the side. Now continue the edge braid as normal. The pair which have been dropped out can be tied and cut short at a later time.

15 Finishing braids

Work until the next pin to be worked is the first pin at the beginning of the braid. A sewing can now be made with each pair matching its own starting point. Leave the workers until last and commence the sewings at the opposite end to the workers. The workers can be attached finally to the last sewing which was worked with the outside pair of passives.

Tie each pair carefully and cut the threads as near to the work as is convenient, to leave a neat row of knots. It is better to tie the second pair from the edge over the outside pair, thus pulling the very outside pair inwards so that their knots will not slip to the outside of the braid when completed. When this is done correctly it is almost impossible to see the join on the right side of the work.

16 Finishing braids (joining to the side of another braid)

Work the braid as far as possible until the next pin has been already worked in the braid to which this one will be attached. Sew in the passives to the threads of the first braid using the worker threads round the pins as much as possible. It is possible to sew into some of the passives as well, but use as few of these as possible. Sew in the worker pair last, tie and cut the threads short.

17 Finishing at a point

This is a useful way of making a neat point although it is recommended that when the point is not attached to any other part of the lace, it should (if possible) be used as a starting and not a finishing point. Work the braid until there are no pinholes left to work. Threads should have been discarded as the braid became narrower so that at this point there are only two pairs of passives left. Now work in whole stitch back through the two passives and leave the workers to the side. Tie each of the passives once. Turn the pillow round through 180 degrees and lay the passives back on top of the finished lace just worked. Take the workers and pass one of them under the passives to make a bunch. Tie the workers together two or three times and cut the threads short, ensuring that the bunch of threads is folded over and lies on top of the work. Remember that this is the underneath when the finished lace is removed from the pillow.

18 Finishing Torchon lace

If the lace has been commenced as recommended in Technique 4 (p. 24), this join can be as neat as joined braids. Work up to and including the final row of pins before the corner diagonal. Each pair of bobbins is now hanging ready as if the work is about to be commenced. Twist each pair twice and sew in to the pin where they should be joined if it were not the end of the work. Tie once and cut off the threads, leaving about 15 cm (6 in).

When the lace has been removed from the pillow, darn in each thread neatly for about 1.5 cm ($\frac{3}{4}$ in) making sure that the darnings are worked in both directions. Cut the thread short. This is a little tedious when a large number of pairs of bobbins has been used, but really essential to do well if the finished lace is to be used and laundered regularly. It has been said that it is not necessary to darn the ends in but just to cut the threads close to the knots and put a dab of fabric adhesive on the knot. This is probably satisfactory as a short-term policy but not over a long period of usage.

19 Normal sewings

The intention of a sewing is to join two pieces of work together whilst still working the second piece. Work until the pin that is used for both sections of work is reached. Now take out this pin. Insert a fine crochet hook into the loop made by the pin and the worker round it, and draw one of the

threads of the worker pair from the second piece through this loop (diagram 20a). Now pass the other worker through the thread that has been pulled through (diagram 20b). Tighten both threads and replace the pin. Now continue the work. Although not indicated in the diagram, it is better to thread the head of the bobbin through the loop first and not the end with the spangles.

The crochet hook which is needed for this technique, and for all the patterns in this book, is the finest that can be purchased. This would be 0.60 (metric), 6 (British), 14–13 (American).

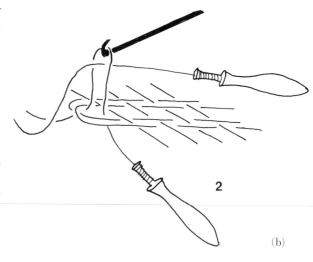

(a)

Diagram 20 Normal sewing

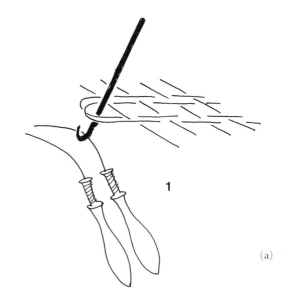

(b)

20 Raised sewings

A raised sewing is worked when the second piece of work is to be joined to a straight edge on the first piece of work. These are usually worked when the two pieces of lace are joined over a certain length at every pinhole. A raised line of threads is formed on the right side of the lace, although this is not seen until the work is finished. When reaching the place when the sewing is to be made, take the pin out and insert the crochet hook into the side of the straight edge, not the edge itself. Diagram 21 shows where this is. Pull through and thread the second bobbin through the first as for normal sewings. Replace the pin.

kers three times. Pass both bobbins of the worker pair over the twisted unworked passives, behind and round the thick pin, and now pass both bobbins under both of the bobbins of the twisted passives.**

Work out to C and back towards B. Now work from ** to ** again and out to D and back. Repeat this movement until all the outside pins have been worked and the next pin is H. The number of outside pins varies according to the pattern. Work a whole stitch with the inside twisted passives. Put in pin H and twist the workers twice. Now *take out the pivot pin B*. The threads that have been piling up this pin should fall flat. Wriggle the passive pair and workers so that the corner is neat, and continue the braid.

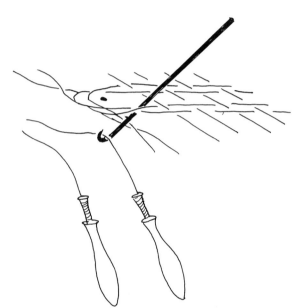

Diagram 21 Raised sewing

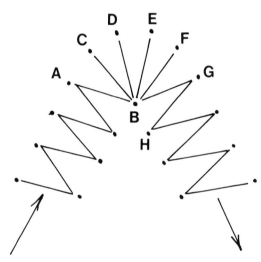

Diagram 22 Working a pivot pin

21 Working a pivot pin

This is always used to turn a sharp corner neatly and when commencing or finishing a Bruges scroll (see Technique 5, p. 24). Work the braid normally until pin B in diagram 22 is reached. This will now be called the pivot pin. Do not work the last pair of passives on row A-B.

Using a thicker pin than for the rest of the work, put in this pin at B with the unworked passives between the pin and the edge of the work. Twist these passives from three to five times according to the distance between the pin before the pivot pin and the following pinhole. **Now twist the wor-

22 Working a pin twice

When the braid is gently curving, there is no need to work a pivot pin, but working several pins twice will give a neat finish to the work. This is done in the following way. Work the pin in the normal way the first time, but do not twist the passives next to the pin. When it is reached the second time, work it as for pin B in Technique 2 (p. 23). There is no need to take the pin out.

On the wrong side of the work, which is uppermost on the pillow, there is a small loop at this point, but the right side of the lace is flat and neat.

23 Crossing braids

When crossing braids there are usually four pins which are used twice. In diagram 23 they are called A, B, C and D. The first line of braid is worked normally. The second line of braid is only attached to the first braid at two of these four pins: the first pin (A) and the diagonally opposite pin (D), or last pin. In the diagram, braid M–N is worked first and then braid O–P. This means that sewings are worked at pins A and D but pins B and C are used a second time without removing them or attaching the two pieces of braid in any way. It is advisable to remove any pins from M–N that will lie under O–P before working the crossing as their removal at a later date could damage the finished lace.

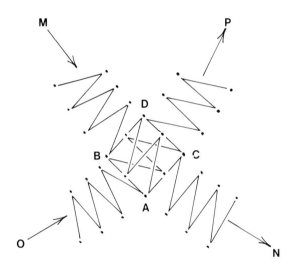

Diagram 23 Crossing braids

24 Joining threads

It is inevitable when working large pieces of lace or long lengths of braid, that threads are going to run out. New threads can be joined in quite easily in one of two ways, depending on the type of pattern being worked and where the threads are in relation to that pattern.

If the piece of lace being worked is a whole-stitch braid or the threads run out whilst a whole-stitch block is being worked, the new thread can be tied with a knot to the end of the old, and incorporated in the finished lace, providing that the knot is eased into place on the reverse side of the

work with the ends sticking out of the work and not woven in.

When threads run short whilst working an open piece of lace or a filling, another method is best used because the knot would leave an untidy bulge in the finished lace. Of course, it is strongly advisable to check on the length of thread needed for fillings before commencing them so that new threads should rarely be required. Either wind enough thread on to the bobbin which has just become empty or fill the bobbin completely if there is a large amount of work still to be done. Hang the new thread on a pin about 5 cm (2 in) above the place where the work has reached. Now weave it through the pins in the work until it reaches the point where the short thread lies. Wind the short thread on the bobbin, together with the new thread, and use them jointly as a single thread for several stitches. The short end can then be discarded and both ends can be cut short on completion of the lace.

25 Using a gimp thread

A gimp thread is one which is thicker than that used for the rest of the lace and it is used to outline or emphasize the design. It can be either of the same colour or a different colour but the most important point is that it must always be three or four times the thickness of the rest of the threads used. If thinner than this, its effect is minimized and much effort in using it has been wasted.

A gimp can be used in conjunction with a thread of the rest of the lace to form a pair of bobbins but this use is normally restricted to fine Honiton or Continental laces. The fine Bruges flower work uses the gimp in this fashion. When it is used to outline a shape within the pattern of the lace, it is woven over and under the normal threads in a separate movement. Once woven through the threads, they must be twisted in order to hold the gimp thread firmly in place.

When two gimps cross one another, they are usually passed right over left as when crossing a normal pair of bobbins. When they weave through a pair of bobbins, the movement is as follows:

1 Twist the pair of bobbins once.

2 Pass the gimp thread under the right thread and over the left, if it is travelling from right to left; pass it over the left thread and under the right if it is travelling from left to right.

3 Now twist the pair of normal threads twice.

There is a school of thought which believes the gimp is passed over the right and under the left thread. This method is just as good. The important thing to remember is that whichever method is used, it must be adhered to throughout that piece of work. Do not change methods in mid-stream.

26 Stiffening the finished lace

It is sometimes necessary to stiffen a finished piece of lace before removing it from the pillow. For example, the Christmas star (pattern 5, p. 53) and the fish and weed in the aquarium (pattern 7, p. 58) needed to be stiffened. There are two methods of doing this, and the lacemaker should decide before commencing her work which method she will employ.

If spray starch is to be used to stiffen the lace, there are two very important points to note. The pattern must be covered by a sheet of greaseproof or tracing paper *before* any lace is worked, and all the edge pins must remain *in situ*. Spray starch gives an excellent finish but the lace and pattern are considerably dampened during the process. The ink markings on the pattern can easily mark the finished work and completely spoil the lace, hence the layer of greaseproof paper between pattern and lace. The edge pins must be retained in order to keep the lace shape correct until the starch has completely dried. This process takes a few hours and the work should be left overnight if possible to dry.

Non-perfumed hair lacquer makes an excellent substitute for the traditional starch. Although it is best to leave all the edge pins in place, it is not vital. Nor is the greaseproof paper necessary as the work is not dampened to such an extent. At the present time, there are no obvious disadvantages in using hair lacquer, but, of course, it has not been on the market long enough to give it the full test of time. Only the passing of the years will do this.

27 Mounting pictures

Many lacemakers believe this to be a difficult task and so shy away from working pictures. This need not be the case. When attaching a piece of lace to a backing material it is extremely important to ensure that, firstly, the original shape is adhered to and, secondly, that there are no wrinkles in the backing material. The actual backing material can be of almost any type of fabric or even card or paper. Which type or colour one should use depends upon the colour of the lace and what the motif depicts. Hence the ballerina in silver and white (pattern 16, p. 108) demanded a rich background of purple velvet and the winter scene of the robin (pattern 17, p. 112) needed the cold effect produced by grey felt.

If only using card as a mount, the lace can be attached by using very small dabs of PVA fabric adhesive at suitable places. Extreme care must be taken, though, to ensure that the adhesive is not used too liberally and that it does not mark the card. Hence, this method is not really recommended as many hours of laborious lacemaking can be ruined in a minute.

The ideal method is to sew the motif or picture to material. This need not be time consuming if approached in the correct manner. First, it must be ensured that there is ample backing material. Do not be skimpy over this. There must be enough to mount the lace and to fold over the reverse side of the finished mount as well. Use an embroidery frame and put the backing material into it. Make sure it is stretched as tight as possible in all directions and that any warp and weft are at right angles to one another. Now put the lace on the material and pin it lightly into place. It is now a relatively simple task to sew the lace into place using a needle threaded with the same thread as that which made the lace. If the edges only are sewn and the stitches are worked into the loops made by the edge pins, the stitching will be virtually invisible. If there are other points of lace not attached within the design, these must also be caught to the backing material with a small stitch. On removal of the finished picture from the embroidery frame, it will be seen that this is a very neat, effective method. It is not usually necessary to attach the centre part of the lace to the backing material.

The decision should have been made earlier as to the type of frame chosen for the finished picture or whether, indeed, a frame is to be used at all. If using a photograph frame, consider using the glass as a firm base on which to attach the picture. It is very rigid and the lace can be viewed without the reflection of the glass interfering.

Opposite sides of the backing material are folded over the wrong side of the glass after first ensuring that the lace is positioned in the centre on the right side, and it is then stitched into position with long stitches pulling the two edges together (diagram 24a). This ensures that the material is stretched tightly over the front. Now fold the other two opposite sides over and repeat the exercise (diagram 24b). The finished effect on the front should be smooth and unwrinkled. The picture can then be inserted into the frame and the back clipped on.

Hardboard and thin plywood also make ideal bases for a picture. Make sure, though, that the edges are sanded thoroughly and smoothly. The backing material can then be attached in the same manner as for photograph frames, or even glued into place with PVA fabric adhesive. If any other type of adhesive is used, make sure that none touches the right side of the picture. To give a neat finish to the wrong side, another piece of backing material which is slightly smaller than the finished picture can be sewn or glued over the back.

Diagram 24 Back of a picture

(a)

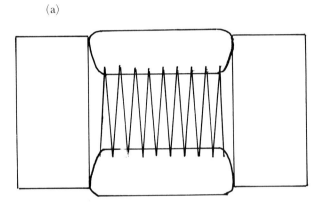

(b)

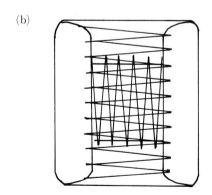

28 Dealing with large numbers of bobbins

There are, inevitably, some designs which demand a large number of bobbins and it is always a problem to dispose of those not in use in order to have a clear space on the pillow for working. The two best ways of disposing of idle bobbins are 'bundling' and 'layering'.

For 'bundling', a number of long divider pins are needed. Hat pins make excellent pins for this purpose. Making sure that the length of thread between bobbins and work is sufficient, take the bobbins from one section of the lace that is not to be worked for a time, and push them round the edge of the work to the back of the pillow. Put a divider pin on both sides of the bunch of bobbins. Alternatively, all the threads in a group of bobbins can be wound round one divider pin all at the same time in one movement. Then the pin is put in the pillow round towards the rear of the work. The only problem with either of these well-tried and tested methods is that, when wishing to use these bobbins again, the lacemaker must spend some time in untwisting the threads.

For the 'layering' method, leave the bobbins lying flat on the pillow each in their appropriate place, but still pushing them round to the rear of the work. When they have filled the space at the side of the work, cover them with a cover cloth and put the next section of bobbins on top of this cloth in sequence until there is no more space. This can be repeated until there are several layers of bobbins. The advantage of this method is that there is no time wasted in discovering the next bobbins to use. But the threads between bobbins and the lace already worked must be long enough or the lace will slide up the pins and away from the pillow and pattern.

5 Filling stitches

There are numerous filling stitches which give a great number of different effects. There is little need for any modern lacemaker to invent any new fillings as the traditional ones are well tried and excellent. The book which describes these fillings thoroughly and which is now used by many lacemakers as their main reference volume is *The Book of Bobbin Lace Stitches*, Bridget M. Cook and Geraldine Stott, B. T. Batsford Ltd, 1980. The way in which to prick these fillings and the methods of working them are fully described by these ladies who have carried out much careful research into the subject. Therefore only a brief outline of the fillings used for the designs in this volume is included for reference. It will be noted that some of the diagrams that follow show the position of each thread while in others, where it is too complex to show each thread, each line represents a pair of bobbins.

Whole-stitch block

Every stitch is worked as a whole stitch and the workers are twisted once or twice after the pin has been put into position and before enclosing it. The threads are all twisted once or twice before joining the block of whole stitch and after leaving it. If they are twisted twice, the block of whole stitch is defined more clearly in the finished work. It is easy to see from the diagram why this filling is called cloth stitch or linen stitch as it resembles a piece of woven material when completed.

Half-stitch block

This is worked in a similar fashion to the whole-stitch block but every stitch is a half stitch. After putting in the pin at the edge of the block, twist the pair of bobbins that are outside it once before commencing the next row of half stitch. This ensures that the same bobbin works across each

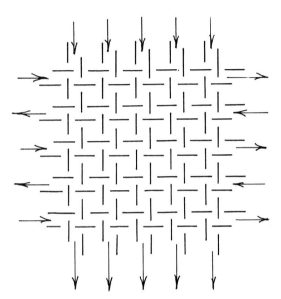

Diagram 25 Whole stitch

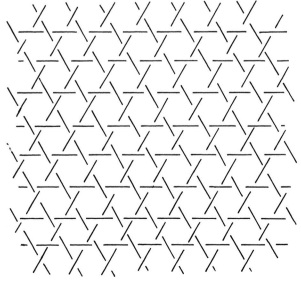

Diagram 26 Half stitch

33

row and it helps to give a neater finish. As for the whole-stitch blocks, it is better to twist the passives at least twice before joining or leaving the block of half stitch.

This is a difficult stitch to keep tidy whilst working it because the bobbins are not kept in their original pairs. If the lacemaker has trouble in deciding whether the passives are in the correct position to commence a row of half stitch, a worthwhile tip is to remember that each pair should be crossed right over left before working the half stitch through them.

Torchon ground

The same movement is worked at each pinhole, proceeding down a diagonal line of work. It is not important whether the left-hand or right-hand lines of work are completed first, but do not try to work back up a line. At each pinhole the bobbins are worked as follows: half stitch, pin, half stitch.

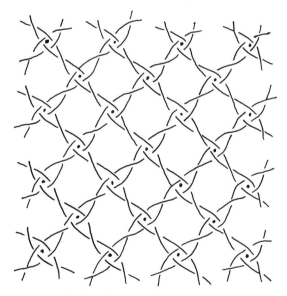

Diagram 27 Torchon ground

Dieppe ground

There is no diagram for this filling stitch. It is worked as for the Torchon ground with the addition of a twist between each stitch. Hence the movement at each pinhole is: half stitch, pin, half stitch, twist both pairs once. The overall effect is similar to Torchon ground but the extra twist gives a neater finish to the completed lace and it does not pull out of shape as easily.

Whole stitch and twist

This stitch is known in France as *fond épingle close* or *tulle du puy*. It gives an attractive appearance and a slight elasticity to the finished lace. Each pinhole is worked: whole stitch, pin, whole stitch, twist both pairs.

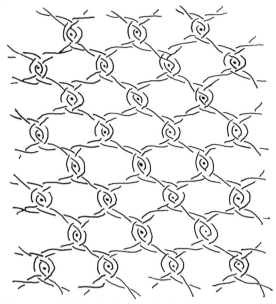

Diagram 28 Whole stitch and twist

Flemish ground

Once again, no diagram is included because of its similarity to the previous filling stitch. Each pinhole is worked: whole stitch, twist each pair three times, pin, whole stitch, and twist each pair three times. This makes the hole formed by the pin larger and gives an extra decorative effect to the lace when finer threads are used.

Rose ground

There are a number of different methods of working rose grounds, each producing an interesting effect, but only one of these is used in this book and so only one is depicted here. Whenever working any of the varieties of rose ground, it is best to devise a system of working and adhere strictly to it. Otherwise, it is sometimes difficult to recall exactly which position has been reached.

Diagram 29 depicts the positions of the threads, whilst in diagram 30 the pinhole arrangements and markings on the pattern are shown. Rose ground is always worked in blocks of four pinholes.

The movements at each block of four are as follows.

1 Before working pinhole 1, take the two left-hand pairs and work a whole stitch and twist. Leave these to one side and now take the two right-hand pairs and work a whole stitch and twist. The threads are now ready to work the four pin block.

2 Using the two centre pairs, work a half stitch, put a pin at 1 and enclose it with a half stitch.

3 Take the two left-hand pairs and work a half stitch, pin and half stitch at hole 2.

4 With the two right-hand pairs, work a half stitch, pin, half stitch at hole 3.

5 And finally, with the two centre pairs, work a half stitch, pin, half stitch at hole 4.

6 Now work a whole stitch and twist with the two left-hand pairs and likewise with the two right-hand pairs.

The block is now completed and the threads are in position to work the next block. Note that it is not necessary to work a whole stitch and twist to commence a four hole block if it has already been worked at the previous block. It is vital to remember this whole stitch and twist, because without it, the essential squareness of this ground is not produced.

Diagram 29 Rose ground thread positions

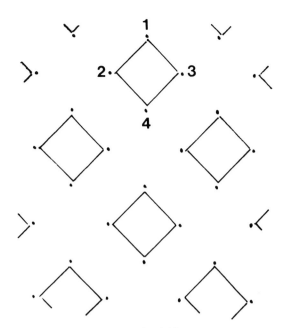

Diagram 30 Rose ground pricking

Plaits and picots

It is usually possible for this filling to be worked with only two pairs of bobbins commencing and finishing at the same place. It is a typical filling for much of the Bruges flower work. The arrows on the diagram show the direction of work for the plaits. Picots are worked at pins B, D, F, G. J, L, M, O, P, and Q. Sewings are worked at pins C and H.

Hang in two pairs of bobbins at A using Technique 10 (p. 26), and work a plait to B where a picot is worked. Now continue the plait to D, putting a pin at C and working the plait round this pin. Work a picot at D and continue the plait to E where a sewing is made into the braid using only one pair of bobbins (see Technique 19, p. 28). If the plait has been worked tightly and continues until it is directly over the pin, there is no need to work a sewing with the second pair. Now continue the plait to F. Make a picot and plait to G, working round pin C. Form a picot at G and continue in this manner.

After working the picots at O and P, the plait will be passing round pins H and C respectively for the last time. Therefore the plaits at these points must be attached to one another. This is done by removing the pin and working a sewing through both the plaits already there before continuing the present plait. The threads are drawn up tightly and the pin is not replaced. Once again, there is no need to work a sewing with the second pair, provided that the plait has been worked tightly. When pin A is reached, the pairs can both be sewn in, tied and the threads cut short.

If careful examination is made of any of the patterns using this filling, it is usually possible to work large sections in this way. If preferred, there is an alternative method of working this filling.

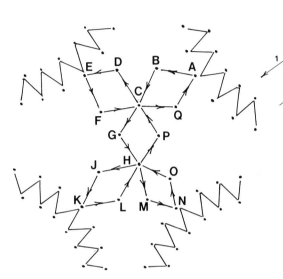

Diagram 31 Plaits and picots

The plaits and picots are worked as an integral part of one of the braids. In diagram 31, for example, the braids which involve pins E, K and N would be worked as normal. When the pin A was reached on that braid, the workers and outside passive pair could be used to complete the filling and then sewn back in at A to complete the braid. This method is very useful as the finished lace does not contain any tied ends which could come adrift with usage.

Honeycomb ground

This is not the true honeycomb ground as worked in English Bucks Point laces, but it is the type used in many European patterns and is known as Scandinavian ground. The pricking is set out at a 45-degree angle to the line of work. The actual movements at each pinhole are the same, though. At every pinhole the movements are: half stitch, twist both pairs, pin, half stitch and twist both pairs once. Referring to diagram 32, work down row 1, up row 2, down row 3, up row 4 etc.

Diagram 32 Honeycomb ground

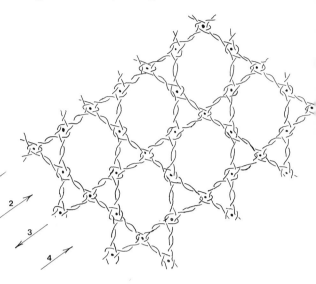

This filling is very economical in time and movement because there is no need to transfer the bobbins continually from the right to left side on the pillow on completing each row of work. Every alternate row is worked upwards using consecutive pairs of bobbins so that, as they are moved across the pillow, they are actually being used to make a stitch.

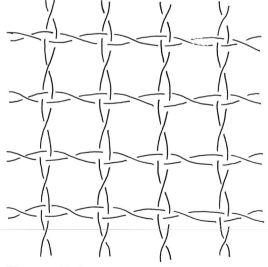

Diagram 33 Gauze ground

Gauze ground

There are no pinholes except at the edge of this ground. If, however, a large area is being worked and the lacemaker has difficulty in keeping the passive pairs straight, pins can be placed at suitable points to assist. At every crossing of the threads, work a whole stitch and twist both pairs once, remembering to twist the workers before the first stitch in each row.

Half-gauze ground

Once again, no pins are required in the centre of this ground. It is worked in a similar fashion to the gauze ground, but the passives are not twisted. This gives a closer effect with a slightly striped appearance, and it is easier to keep the passives straight.

Three-legged spiders

These are also known as plain Torchon spiders, as each leg is attached to the next spider. The diagram does not depict every thread of this ground due to the complexity of showing the twists. Each line represents a pair of bobbins and twists are shown by the short slanting lines across the threads. The number of these lines indicates the number of twists required. The method of working the actual spider is described in the chapter on stitches (see p. 21).

Snowflakes (sunspots)

This filling is normally called 'sunspots' but it is also known as 'snowflakes'. Each set of pinholes needs six pairs of bobbins and is worked in half stitch as a Bedfordshire spider. Plaits are worked between each spider. Diagram 36 shows the order in which the pinholes are worked. For pinhole 1, work a whole stitch with the right-hand pair from plait A and the left-hand pair from plait B. Put in the pin, enclose it with a whole stitch and twist both pairs once. The rest of the snowflake is worked in half stitch.

Row 1–2 Using the left-hand pair from pin 1 as workers, work across the left-hand pair from A and both pairs from C before putting in pin 2 – four pairs of passives.

Row 2–3 Work across the pairs already incorporated, adding in the second pair from plait B – five pairs of passives.

Row 3–4 Work across all the pairs.

Row 4–5 Work across all but the last pair – four pairs of passives.

Row 5–6 Work across all but the last pair – three pairs of passives.

Finish by enclosing pin 6 with a whole stitch. Now the three plaits can be formed to work towards the next snowflakes.

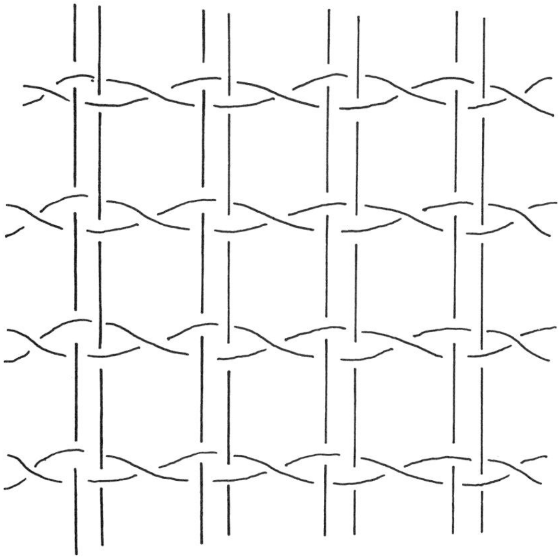

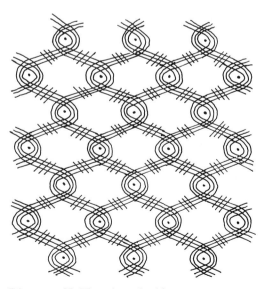

Diagram 34 Half-gauze ground

Diagram 35 Three-legged spiders

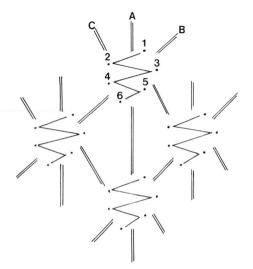

Diagram 36 Snowflakes (sunspots)

Whole-stitch clover ground

This is a whole-stitch block with a hole in the centre. After working each pinhole, the workers become passives and the last pair of passives used become the workers. The centre hole is also worked in a similar fashion. Diagram 37 shows the positions of each pair of bobbins. The pinhole at the centre is worked: half stitch, pin, half stitch. Note that all pairs are twisted twice between the blocks and across the centre hole. Working a whole-stitch block in this fashion makes a smoother edge than the normal method.

Lock stitch

It is important to keep the twisted passives straight in this ground, but this is easier to achieve than when working the gauze ground because the workers are anchored in the centre and not only at the edge. At each pinhole work a whole stitch, pin, whole stitch, and twist both pairs once. Then each worker pair passes through the twisted passives on either side with a whole stitch. Twist both pairs once without any pin being used. Diagram 38 shows the positions of each pair of bobbins as this is being worked.

Flower-centred braid

This stitch looks very like latticed windows when finished; the whole stitch at the joining of the plaits forms a block that gives the appearance of a blob of lead as found in this type of window. Plaits are worked between each set of four pinholes. The worker for each block is the right-hand pair of the right-hand plait. Put a pin between the two pairs of the right-hand plait before working through the other three passives in whole stitch. Twist the workers once round the outside of the pin and work back through the passives twice more. The two right-hand pairs of passives are now plaited to the next group of pinholes and a pin is put in the last hole between the left-hand pairs before they are plaited similarly.

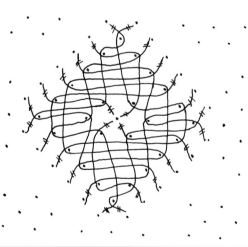

Diagram 37 Whole-stitch clover ground

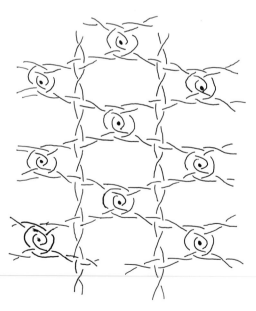

Diagram 38 Lock stitch

1 Table lamp

2 Winter scene

3 Wedding medallion

4 Monogram badge

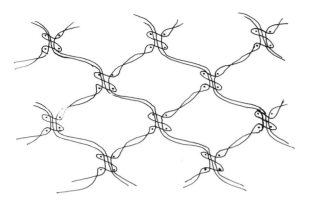

Diagram 39 Flower-centred braid

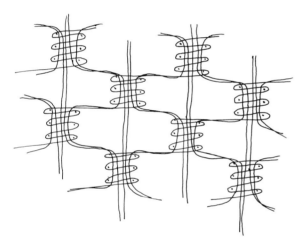

Diagram 40 Brick and braid ground

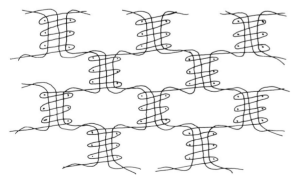

Diagram 41 Devonshire wall filling

Brick and braid ground

Plaits are worked between each set of six pinholes which uses six pairs of bobbins and is worked in whole stitch, twisting the workers twice outside each pin. The worker for each block is the right-hand pair of the right-hand plait. It works through all the other pairs before the first pin is inserted. The line of work is indicated in diagram 40. Note that the plaits leaving the blocks do not use the same pairs of bobbins as the plaits before the blocks.

Devonshire wall filling

Each set of six pinholes needs four pairs of bobbins and is worked in whole stitch. Use the right-hand pair of the right-hand plait as workers and twist them twice outside each pin. The pairs are not plaited between the blocks. The right-hand pairs are worked in one whole stitch. For the left-hand pairs, pass the worker pair under the other pair and then work a whole stitch with them. The threads are now ready to work the next blocks.

Whole-stitch blocks

Each set of six pinholes uses four pairs of bobbins. The pairs are plaited between each set. The top centre pin is worked first. Using the left-hand pair from the right-hand plait, and the right-hand pair from the left-hand plait, work a whole stitch. Twist both pairs once, put in the pin and enclose it with a whole stitch. Work a whole stitch with the left-hand pair and the other pair from the left-hand plait, and leave. Now take the right-hand pair from the right-hand plait and use it to work through all the other pairs which will now become the passives for the following four pinholes. Twist the workers twice outside each pin and leave to the left after completing the block. A whole stitch is now worked with the two right-hand passives. Work another whole stitch using the middle two pairs of bobbins. Put a pin in the last pinhole, twist these two pairs once and enclose the pin with a whole stitch. The two plaits can now be worked to the next set of pinholes. It will be noted that the workers are not twisted as many times as is normal for this filling, but in the context in which it was used for the pattern in this book (the lighthouse, pattern 20, p. 126) it was both unnecessary and undesirable to do any more twists.

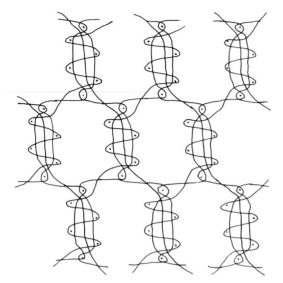

Diagram 42 Whole-stitch blocks

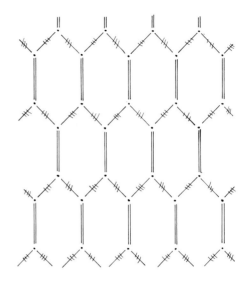

Diagram 44 Braided net

Pea with braid filling

Plaits are worked between each set of six pinholes which requires four pairs. Work these plaits across one another in whole stitch. Taking the two pairs to the left, use the right-hand pair to work in whole stitch backwards and forwards across the other pair, putting in a pin after each crossing, and twisting this worker pair twice outside the pin. Similarly use the left-hand pair of the two pairs to the right to work the other three pinholes. Now cross the four pairs as at the beginning of the block and work plaits to the next blocks of pinholes.

Braided net

A plait is worked between each vertical pair of pinholes and the pairs are separated to form the next plaits. Each pair is twisted three times between each plait. This is one more than is usual in this filling, but the context in which it is used in this book (the roof of the lighthouse pattern 20, p. 136) required this. Pins are not always inserted at each end of the plaits, but it was necessary in this instance because the filling was pricked out on polar graph paper to obtain the required effect.

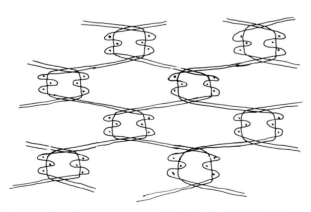

Diagram 43 Pea with braid filling

6 THE PATTERNS

The following 20 patterns use traditional stitches and techniques, combined with modern adaptations and threads, to achieve lace that can be put to practical use in the home. The instructions assume that the lacemaker will be familiar with the basic stitches and techniques, and each pattern is accompanied by a black and white photograph of the finished result, a pricking which is the correct size and can be photocopied or traced direct from the book and, in many cases, a working diagram.

1 Silhouette

This pattern was originally designed to be inserted into a white oval china frame, but many different subjects can be treated in a similar fashion for various finished locations.

Dimensions
12·5 × 14 cm high (5 × 5½ in)

Materials required
50 DMC Retors d'Alsace thread in white
15 pairs of bobbins
piece of black felt
white backing material

Figure 5 Silhouette:
an outline of a lady in black
felt with white lace decorations

Diagram 45 Silhouette: outline for black felt

Bottom skirt section

Hang eight pairs of bobbins along the end of the bottom braid and seven pairs along the top. The bottom braid is worked in half stitch with the exception of the edges. The hem is a row of picots followed by two whole stitches. Four half stitches and one whole stitch are then worked to complete the row. The other braid is made up of: two whole stitches, twist the workers once, two whole stitches, twist the workers once, two whole stitches. When using the two pairs of workers for the middle joining stitch: twist each pair five times, work a whole stitch, put the pin in between them, work another whole stitch to enclose the pin and twist each pair five times again.

Top skirt section

This is worked in a similar fashion to the bottom skirt section, except that there are only seven pairs of bobbins for the half-stitch braid and not eight pairs as before. Some of the pins at the waist may need to be worked twice as in Technique 22 (p. 29).

Bodice section

Hang six pairs of bobbins along the end. Picots are worked at the bottom edge only, followed by one whole stitch, four half stitches and one whole stitch to complete the row. A pivot pin will be needed at the inside centre point (see Technique 21, p. 29).

Fan section

Hang six pairs of bobbins along the end. The braid has picots at each side, whilst the rest of it is made up of: two whole stitches, twist the workers once, one whole stitch, twist the workers once, two whole stitches.

The pieces of braid are each worked a little longer than the finished length required. When each braid is completed, the threads may be tied and cut short. The ends of the lace are then folded over the black felt outline and glued into position on the underside only with PVA fabric adhesive. The finished silhouette can then be attached to the backing material and the picture finished.

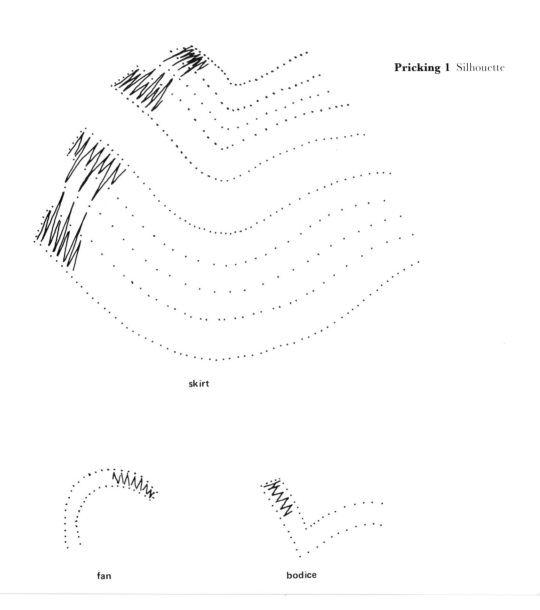

Pricking 1 Silhouette

skirt

fan

bodice

44

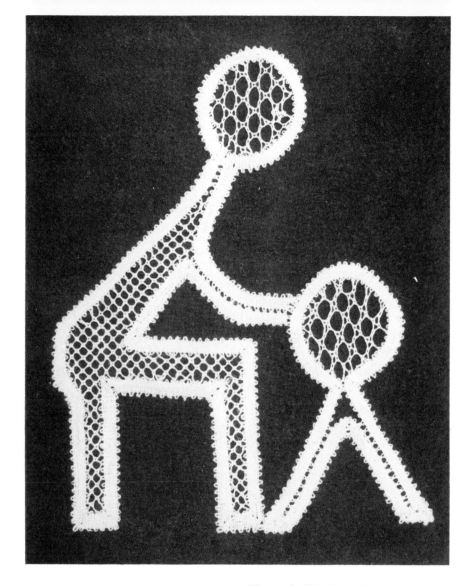

Figure 6a The lacemaker: normal size logo

The lacemaker

This was originally designed as a logo and was made simple with the intention that it could be magnified or reduced when necessary. This is demonstrated by including three patterns. The petite size was used for a paperweight and the miniature for a brooch or tie motif.

Normal size
Dimensions
$13\cdot5 \times 15$ cm ($5\frac{1}{4} \times 6$ in)

Materials required
30 Brillante d'Alsace in required colour
22 pairs of bobbins
Backing material to complement the thread colour

The outside shape is worked in two separate whole-stitch braids using six pairs of bobbins for each. Commence at the base of the pillow and work round the pillow and stand, using a pivot pin (Technique 21, p. 29) at the sharp turns and the double pin (Technique 22, p. 29) at any other bends where necessary. Work sewings as for Technique 19 (p. 28) to join the sides of the stand legs together. Join the braid to the commencement as in Technique 15 (p. 27). The second braid commences at the upper side of the arm at the pillow and continues round the entire body, head and legs of the stool, working sewings at the base of the hand at the pillow. Sewings are also worked at the neck and to join the upper and lower arm sections, and where the leg of the stool meets the

45

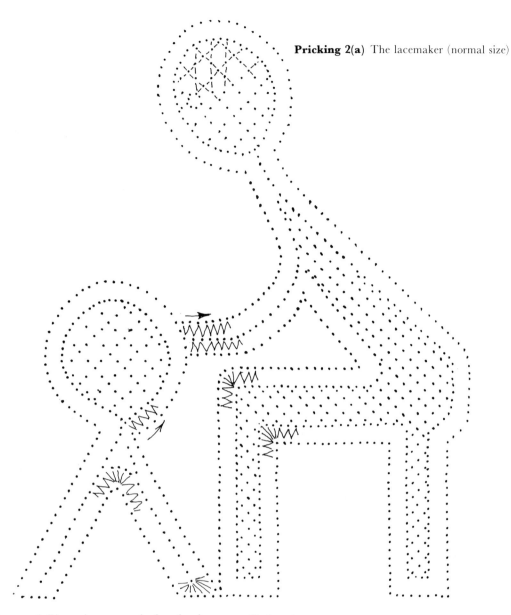

leg of the stand. Pivot pins are worked at the sharp turns.

The pillow filling uses 10 pairs of bobbins and is worked in the honeycomb ground. The bobbins are hung in at the top of the pillow using Technique 10 (p. 26) and are sewn out at the base using Technique 13 (p. 27). The head is also honeycomb filling but using 11 pairs of bobbins. Commence at the top of the head and work a whole-stitch block for the eye when it is reached without adding more pairs of bobbins. The body and stool leg uses 22 pairs of bobbins. It is worked all in one piece, commencing at the neck using Dieppe ground.

Petite size

Dimensions
6 cm ($2\frac{1}{4}$ in) tall

Materials required
DMC Retors d'Alsace 50 or equivalent
six pairs of bobbins
backing material

The original motif was worked in apricot-coloured silk thread and was mounted on a royal blue felt fabric. Five pairs of bobbins are needed for the braid outline and an extra pair to work the centre of the pillow. Pivot pins are worked at all the sharp

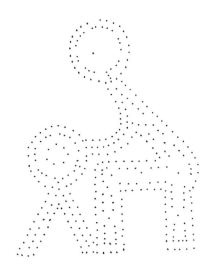

bends and normal sewings are worked where the braids meet.

Miniature size

Dimensions
3 cm ($1\frac{1}{4}$ in) tall

Materials required
120 Honiton cotton thread
six pairs of bobbins

This is worked in a similar fashion to the petite size motif, but all the outside edges are worked as straight edges. It will also be noted that the centre of the pillow does not need an extra pair of bobbins.

Pricking 2(b) The lacemaker (petite size)

Pricking 2(c) The lacemaker (miniature size)

Figure 6b The lacemaker: petite size in a paperweight

Figure 6c The lacemaker: miniature size on a tie

3 Woollen scarf

This scarf is very cosy and warm to wear and can be adapted for any length. There is no need to stiffen or starch the lace in any way as the woollen threads hold their shape extremely well if pulled firmly round the pins. Beware, however, of pulling the passives in the edge braid too tightly as they will pucker up if there is too much tension put upon them. If desired, this design could be worked in a thick linen thread and used with great effect as a dressing table or sideboard runner.

Dimensions
$22 \cdot 5 \times 115$ cm ($8\frac{3}{4} \times 45$ in)

Materials required
2×25 g balls of Patons Beehive
2-Ply Baby Wool or equivalent
60 pairs of bobbins (preferably large ones)

Method of working

The scarf is worked in straightforward Torchon lace with Dieppe ground. There are alternate blocks of whole and half stitch in every other row, interspersed with four-legged spiders and rose ground. The edge braid is untwisted whole stitch with the workers twisted twice round the outside pins. To commence, hang one pair of bobbins on each pin with the exception of the pins at each edge of the side braids where two pairs are hung. Now work two rows of whole stitch the complete width of the scarf through all the pairs before commencing the pattern. Repeat the pattern 12 times, or to the required length, then work another two rows of whole stitch across the entire width. Tie the threads in pairs and leave about 5 cm (2 in) of thread to form a fringe.

The fringe for the other end is made by cutting lengths of thread 12 cm (5 in) long and knotting them in pairs with even ends into each loop at the beginning of the scarf.

Note
It is advisable to use large bobbins for this pattern as otherwise too little wool can be wound on at a time. It is best to use a bolster pillow for this design if the lacemaker does not wish to be lifting her pattern frequently. The polystyrene pillows with detachable central squares are, unfortunately, of little use due to the width of the pattern.

Figure 7 Woollen scarf: warmth in lace for a cold day

Pricking 3 Woollen scarf

one pattern repeat

½ st.

½ st.

½ st.

½ st.

½ st.

½ st.

4 Lampshade cover

The inspiration for this pattern came originally from a Swedish design. The gimp thread chosen was a dark blue to match the furnishings of the room in which the lamp was to be used but any colour could be used. The actual shape of the cover can also be easily adapted for different lampshades and it is a relatively simple design for a novice lacemaker to work.

Dimensions
height of lampshade: 18 cm (7 in)
diameter each end: 9 cm ($3\frac{1}{2}$ in)
diameter at centre: 19 cm ($7\frac{1}{2}$ in)

Materials required
DMC Cordonnet Special 80 in ecru
20 crochet cotton in dark blue
54 pairs of bobbins
Three pairs of bobbins for the gimp thread

Method of working
Commence at the top right-hand corner as per Technique 6 (p. 25). Work a whole-stitch braid along the top edge adding pairs as required for the main body of the lace by using Technique 9 (p. 26). Turn the corner employing Technique 7 (p. 25). Now the lace can be worked downwards adding in pairs as per Technique 9 (p. 26) and using gimps where required. It is best to use the gimp thread double in order to make it thick enough to make a bold outline to the design. The threads are discarded as per Technique 14 (p. 27) after the half-way stage. Finish as per Technique 14 (after turning the corner at the left-hand side).

To assemble
Make six identical sections of lace. Join them together down the sides by oversewing the seams so that the whole-stitch section at the side does not show. Use the same thread that made the lace to sew the pieces together. Omit the final seam that will make the lace into a cylindrical shape. Now place the cover over the lampshade and stretch it into place, pinning it at appropriate places. The final seam can now be made using a flat stitch and the top and bottom edges can be attached to the shade.

Figure 8 Table lamp with lace lampshade cover

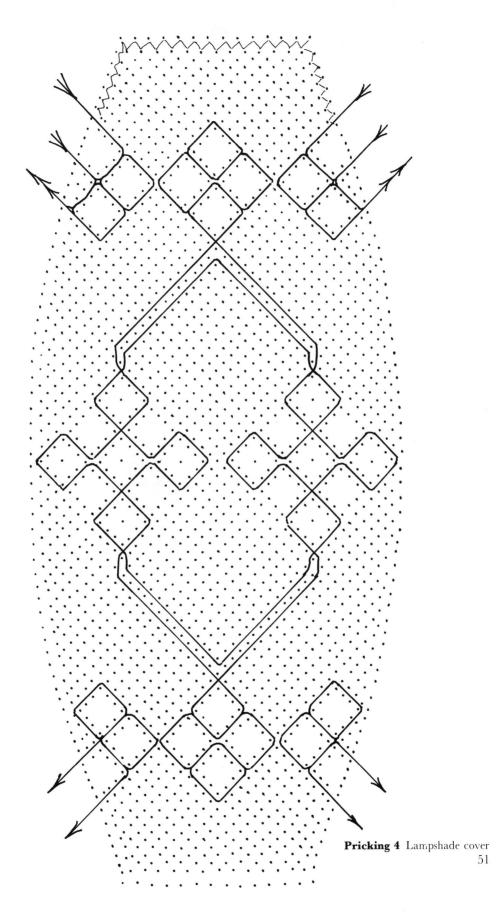

Pricking 4 Lampshade cover

51

Figure 9 Christmas star

5 Christmas star

This is a three-dimensional 12-pointed star Christmas decoration used as a mobile. It can look very attractive when hung over a Christmas tree. The lights reflect the silver edges and give them a frosty appearance.

Dimensions
21·5 cm (8½ in) overall in each direction

Materials required
90 BOUC Fil de Lin in white
DMC Fil Argent
five-amp fuse wire
20 pairs of bobbins

Method of working

Work two pieces of each pattern. The outside braids require five passive pairs of Fil Argent and one worker of 90 BOUC linen. Five-amp fuse wire is added to the outside passive bobbin for strength. The braid is worked in whole stitch, twisting the worker pair once before and once after working the outside passive pair. All the points are worked as pivot pins (see Technique 21, p. 29). The braid leading up to a point loses two pairs of passives as it gets narrower, as in Technique 12 (p. 27). These are picked up again as it widens at the other side using Technique 8 (p. 25).

It is very important *not* to work sewings to join

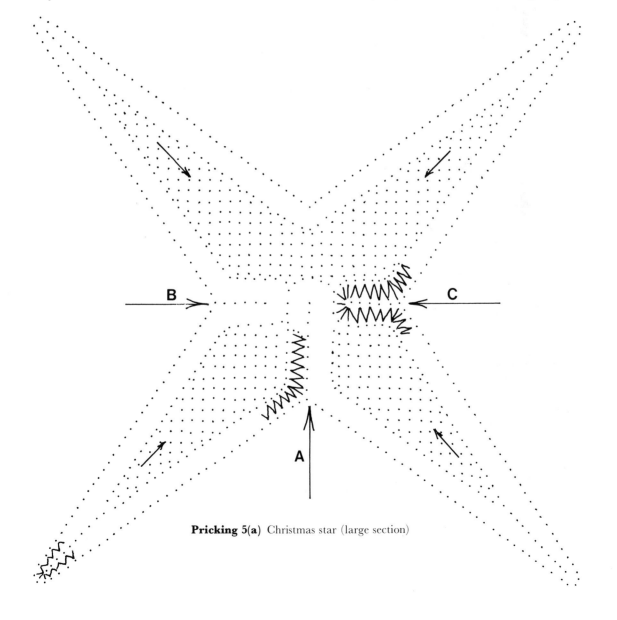

Pricking 5(a) Christmas star (large section)

the braids at slots A, B, C and D. They must be left free in order to assemble the star.

The filling stitch is Dieppe ground worked from the points inwards towards the centre using 90 BOUC linen.

To assemble

To assemble the star, first spray all the pieces to stiffen the lace (see Technique 26, p. 31) before joining them. Slot the two larger pieces together at right angles to one another using the two slots A. Take one of the smaller pieces and insert slot D into slot B. Likewise, using the other smaller piece, insert slot D into slot C. In order to keep the star in its correct shape, the places where the lace slots together can be wired into position with some more five-amp fuse wire. This does not show when completed neatly and the ends cut short. Attach a long strand of wire to the tip of one of the points for hanging.

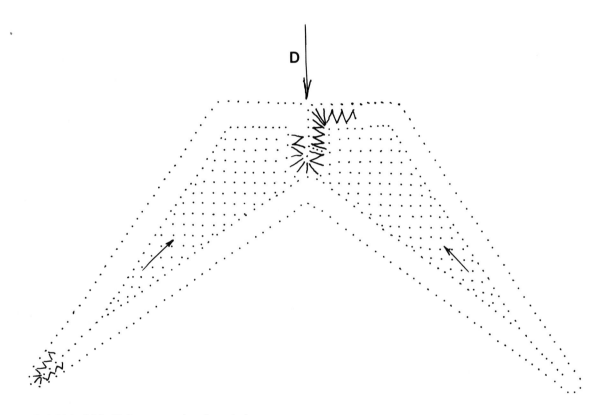

Pricking 5(b) Christmas star (small section)

6 St Valentine's Day mat

This small, octagonal mat has been designed in the style of Bruges flower work. It was inspired by the shape of a lid belonging to a box of chocolates which was a St Valentine's Day gift.

Dimensions
24·5 cm (9¾ in) across

Materials required
90 BOUC Fil de Lin thread or equivalent in white
10 pairs of bobbins

Edge braid

Commence by working the edge braid. Hang ten pairs of bobbins at the place indicated and work the first row as for Technique 1 (p. 23), using half stitch instead of whole stitch. Work the braid in half stitch, ensuring that the edge passives on both sides are worked in whole stitch. Twist both the workers and edge passives once before putting in the pin and also once after enclosing the pin with a whole stitch. Twist the workers twice outside the pin.

Figure 10 St Valentine's Day mat in the style of Bruges flower work

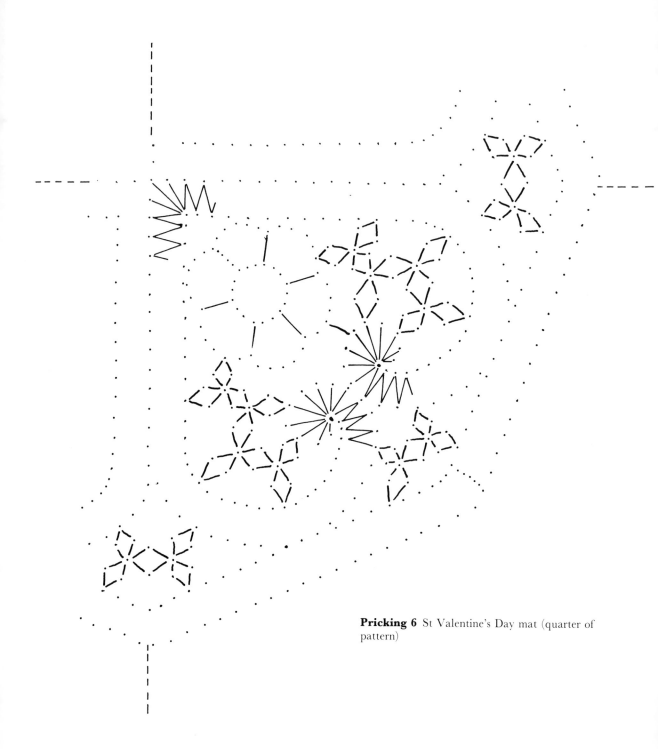

Pricking 6 St Valentine's Day mat (quarter of pattern)

Flowers

Now work the flowers referring to diagram 46. Commence with ten pairs of bobbins on line A-B and work the first line as in Technique 2 (p. 23). Each inner pin is worked twice (see Technique 22, p. 29). Alternate petals are whole and half stitch. The first petal is worked in whole stitch with twists before and after the outer passives at both sides. After line C-D has been worked, twist all the passives once. Now work the second petal in half stitch, ensuring that the edge stitches are still worked in whole stitch and twist. When line E-F has been completed, change back to whole stitch for the next petal, and so on, alternating whole and half stitch for each petal. The last petal is worked in half stitch. Finish the flower using Technique 15 (p. 27).

Scroll braids

Next work the scroll braids. Work a scroll as for Technique 5 (p. 24), increasing to a total of nine passive pairs. the braid is in whole stitch with the workers twisted once before and after each end stitch and twisting the edge passives once. Continue until the point is reached where the braid shares the same pins as the next-door braid. This is point G in diagram 47. Now alter the edge on that side only to a normal foot edge with a change of workers at each pin. The other edge remains the same as before. Continue this foot edge in the same fashion until point J is reached where the braid returns to normal. A pivot pin is worked at H (Technique 21, p. 29). Finish the scroll as described in Technique 5 (p. 24).

When the next door braid is worked, on reaching pin G, the two braids are joined by working raised sewings at each pinhole using Technique 20 (p. 29) until they separate. Work normal sewings where the braids and flowers share a pinhole or where indicated by a line that they should be attached to one another.

Filling

The filling is the plait and picot ground (p. 35).

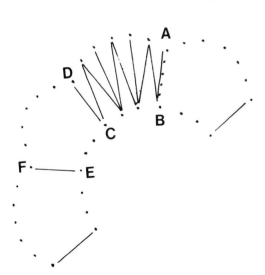

Diagram 46 Bruges flower for St Valentine's Day mat

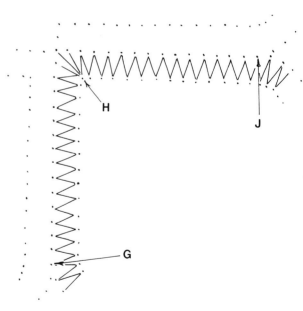

Diagram 47 St Valentine's Day mat: joining braids with raised sewings

7 Aquarium

This is an ideal design for a newcomer to three-dimensional patterns. The shapes are all simple but the overall effect is quite eye-catching and colourful. It is better to use a fish tank that has been used rather than a brand new one because there is usually a watermark or other scratch marks on the surface of an older tank that gives the onlooker an impression of reality.

Dimensions
30 × 18 × 20·5 cm (12 × 7 × 8 in) high approximately

Materials required
1 fish tank
invisible thread
shirring elastic
coarse sandpaper
various small stones

DMC Coton Perle No. 12; colours 906, 580 and 937
DMC Brillante d'Alsace No. 30; colour 947 (orange)

Weed 1

Five pairs of bobbins are needed. Work in whole-stitch braid using one of the Coton Perle No. 12 colours. Commence each leaf at the tip and do not sew in the leaves to one another where they share the same pinholes but keep them separate. End at the roots and leave long threads to attach the weed to the sandpaper floor.

Figure 11 Aquarium: these fish need no food nor does the tank need cleaning out

Weed 2

This uses between six and eight pairs of bobbins. Work in whole-stitch braid with a straight edge, using the second of the Coton Perle No. 12 colours. Once again, commence at the tip of each leaf and do not work sewings where the leaves share the same pins. Finish as for Weed 1.

Weed 3

This weed uses up to eight pairs of bobbins and the third green Coton Perle No. 12 thread. Each leaf is commenced at the tip and is worked in whole-stitch/half-stitch blocks, ensuring that the half-stitch side has a whole stitch and twist at the outside edge. End the leaves with plaited stems and keep long ends as on the other two weeds.

Goldfish

Commence at the nose of each fish and work the main body in whole stitch with straight edges either side, adding in pairs using Technique 8 (p. 25) as required to keep the fabric closely woven. The eye is formed by putting a pin in at Point A (refer to diagram 48) and working two rows of whole stitch using different workers either side of the eye. These workers join with a whole stitch at pin B and only one of them is used for the rest of the fish's body. The other worker becomes a passive again.

Pricking 7 Aquarium weed 1

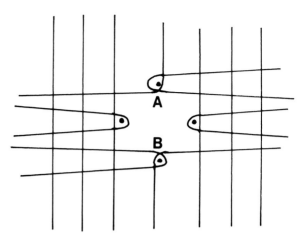

Diagram 48 Aquarium: method of working the fish's eye

When the tail section is reached, twist the workers once between each whole stitch and gradually lose threads as in Technique 12 (p. 27). Finish at single pins using Technique 17 (p. 28).

The lower fins are worked in half stitch, commencing with the part furthest from the body and working raised sewings to join them to the

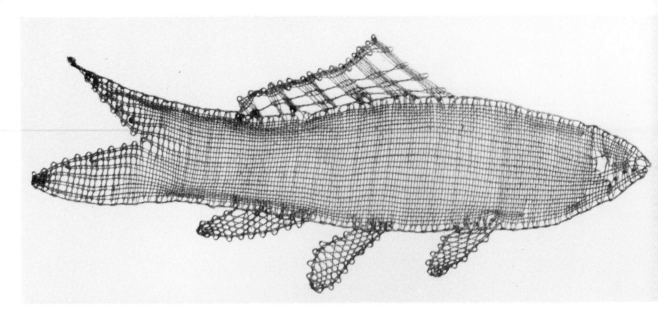

body (see Technique 20, p. 29). The upper fins are worked in whole stitch with twists. Refer to figure 12 which shows this in more detail.

Mounting
Stiffen each piece of lace as in Technique 26 (p. 31). Attach a length of invisible thread to the tip of each leaf and to the top of each fish at the nose, fin and tail. Lay the sandpaper in the base of the tank

Figure 12 Enlargement of the goldfish in the aquarium

Pricking 8 Aquarium weed 2

and position the stones in order that the weeds appear to be growing directly out of them. Stitch the weed roots through the sandpaper and tie them on the underside. Make a mesh of invisible thread to fit over the tank. This can be done by marking the shape of the tank top on to a piece of card and pinning this card to the lace pillow. Run a double length of shirring elastic round thick pins which mark the corners of the tank and now weave a mesh of invisible thread backwards and forwards, making knots at the places where the threads cross one another. When taken off the pillow, slip the shirring elastic edges of the mesh over the top lip of the fish tank. The threads attached to the tips of the weeds can now be tied into position on the top mesh, thus holding the weed upright. The goldfish are suspended from the top mesh to give the impression that they are swimming between the weeds.

Pricking 9 Aquarium weed 3

Pricking 10 Aquarium goldfish

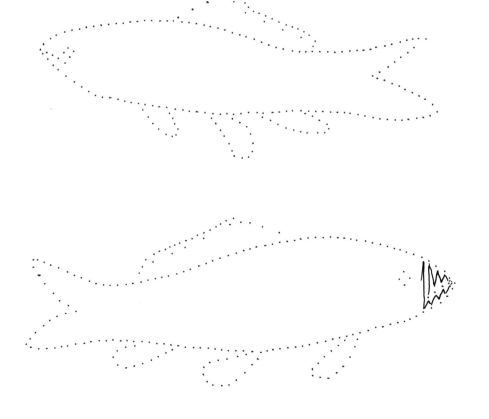

Pictures of animals for the nursery or a child's bedroom are very attractive subjects for the lacemaker. They can be made as simple or as complicated as desired, and the colouring can be adjusted to suit any personal preferences. The two patterns that follow show how very simple outlines can be transferred into loveable animals with a personality of their own. The elephant design, or 'Heffalump' as he is called, is suitable for a novice lacemaker to attempt; while 'Mr Bunny' is a little more complicated, but both have their own appeal and could suggest further subjects for the lacemaker to attempt.

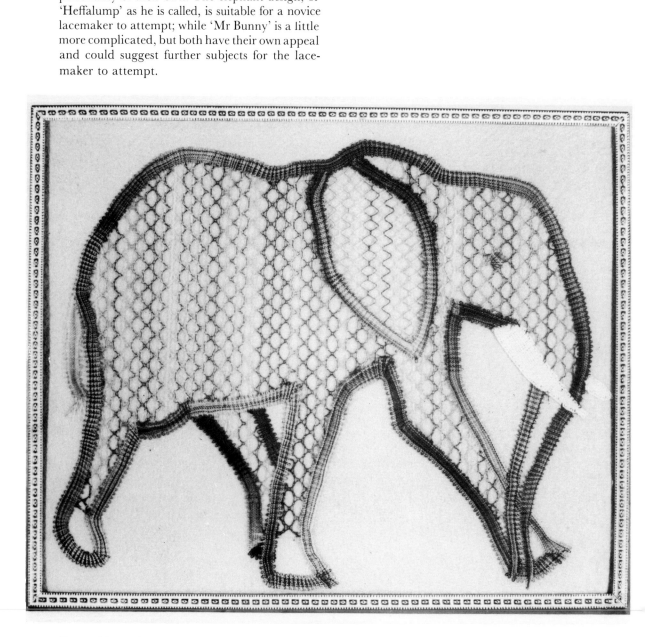

Figure 13 An elephant picture, known as 'Heffalump'

8 'Heffalump'

Dimensions
23·5 × 19 cm (9¼ × 7½ in)

Materials required
Campbells Irish Linen 70 in white
DMC Brillante d'Alsace 30 in variegated grey
45 pairs of bobbins
backing material

Method of working

The two halves of the pattern must first be joined on line a—b. Now commence with the front tusk. Using the white linen thread, hang on three pairs of bobbins at the tip and work in whole stitch, adding more pairs as in Technique 8 (p. 25) to keep the fabric firm and close. End at the point where the tusk joins the head but do not cut and tie the threads yet. The main outline of the elephant is commenced at the end of the trunk. It is worked in whole-stitch braid using six pairs of passives in the variegated grey thread. Work both sections of the trunk simultaneously. The pinholes that are shared are worked as a whole stitch, pin, whole stitch, using the workers from each side. The rear section of the trunk is sewn into the front tusk using Technique 16 (p. 27). The front section continues across the front tusk, working a braid crossing as for Technique 23 (p. 30), and then continuing round the entire body and legs in the direction of the arrows. Pivot pins (Technique 21, p. 29) are worked at the sharp bends and some of the pins are worked twice round the more gentle curves using Technique 22 (p. 29). Braid crossings are made where the front leg passes across the trunk. Finish at the front tusk and tie the ends of the tusk together with the thread ends from the body.

The rear tusk can now be worked and sewn into the head. Next, work the rear leg braids by hanging in the threads at the underside of the body and finishing at the front leg. The tail is a whole-stitch braid as for the body outline, commencing at the top and finishing with the threads forming a short tassel. Do not sew the end of the tail into the leg. The braid for the ear is worked as for the outline and tail.

The filling for the ear is worked in the variegated grey in Dieppe ground, commencing at the top and adding or losing pairs of bobbins as required. The filling for the rest of the elephant is honeycomb ground worked on a 45-degree angle. Once again, commence at the top parts of the body and finish at the under side. When the eye is reached, work a whole-stitch block with the threads already in use. There is no need to add further threads. By judicious planning of the threads, they can be arranged to form darker sections of lace for the rear parts of the body and shadings for other sections. It would also have been a better idea, perhaps, to have used a plain grey thread for the worker pair on the outside braid rather than the same variegated one, so losing the slight 'tartan' effect that the original picture has.

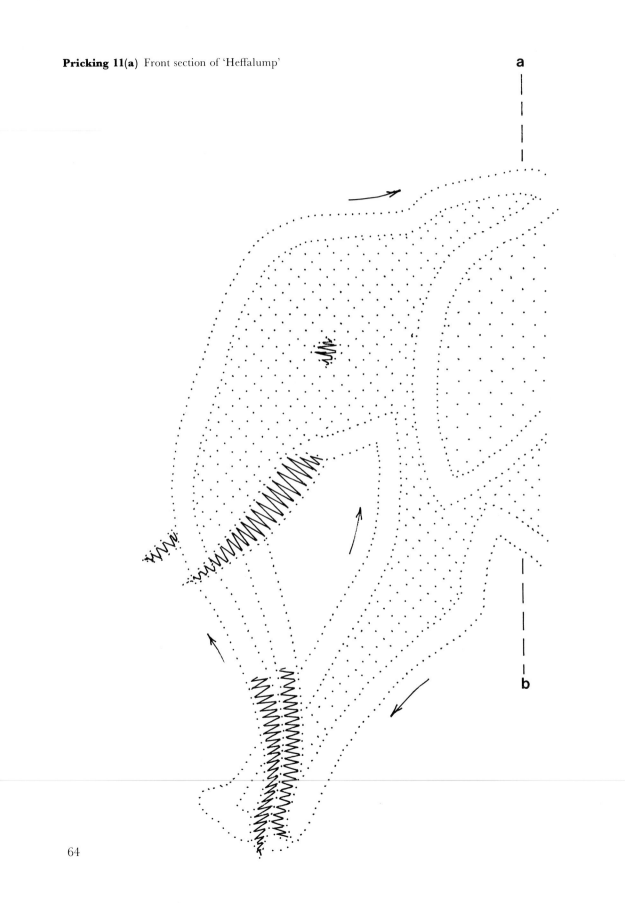

a

b

a

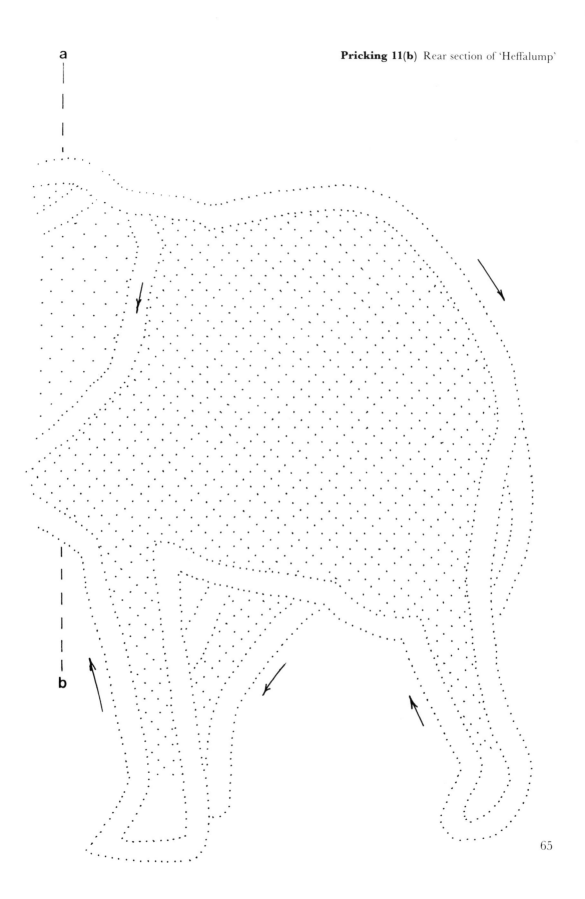

b

65

Figure 14 'Mr Bunny': a charming rabbit with his umbrella

9 'Mr Bunny'

The rabbit motif relies on using different coloured threads to produce the effect of depth and working the filling stitches in different directions to shape the forearm and underbody. He is a little more difficult to work than 'Heffalump', but the overall finished product is extremely pleasing.

Dimensions
15 × 21 cm (6 × 8¼ in)

Materials required
DMC Brillante d'Alsace 30 in the following colours:black, white, ecru, pale fawn (842), dark fawn (841), light blue (827), dark blue (996)
backing material
14 pairs of bobbins

Nose and whiskers

These are worked in black in conjunction with the face outline. Refer to diagram 49 for details. Hang four pairs of bobbins on each of the whisker ends and work plaits as far as the nose. Note that the plait from D is worked before the face outline and the plait from C is commenced at the face outline. Work a whole-stitch block for the nose, starting at the point where the plait from A joins, and ending at the bottom. Lose two pairs of bobbins every row (see Technique 12, p. 27). Tie the remaining pairs in a bundle as for finishing at a point (Technique 17, p. 28).

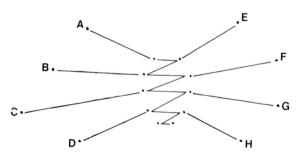

Diagram 49 Nose and whiskers of rabbit

Face and ears

Starting at the base of the front ear, hang on five pairs of bobbins using the dark fawn thread number 841. Work in whole-stitch braid up the ear, down the other side using a pivot pin to turn the point at the top (Technique 21, p. 29), then down the neck and chin, working a sewing where

the whisker from C commences. Now follow the chin over the nose, working a braid crossing as for Technique 23 (p. 30) and finally up the front of the head and front ear, working normal sewings (see Technique 19, p. 28) as the ear tip is reached. Tie off and lay the threads over the braid just worked to join in for the rear ear. Sew in to the top of the head when this outline is complete.

Body and legs

Work the rest of the outline in the following order using five pairs of bobbins as for the face and ears in thread 841.

1 Work the front arm commencing at the underarm.

2 Work the front of the chest using the threads laid over the arm braid as for the ears.

3 Now the back leg can be worked commencing at the haunch and working right round the rear and up to the back of the neck. Work double pins where necessary (Technique 22) at the sharp curves.

4 The underbelly section and rear front paw can now be worked. The back leg cannot be made until after the umbrella has been completed.

Tail

Using white thread and five pairs of bobbins, join in at the top and work the braid outline sewing in at the base. The filling is the whole stitch and twist ground. Work the filling in white, commencing at the top and adding or losing pairs as necessary.

Umbrella

The handle is worked in black and the material part in dark blue, number 996. Each section of the handle is commenced at the bottom and worked towards the paw. Six pairs are needed and it is worked in whole stitch with a straight edge on either side. Note that the rounded end of the handle is started with only four pairs of bobbins and two more are added as required. The material section of the umbrella is now worked. Firstly the four top folds are made. They are worked in whole-stitch blocks, using seven pairs of bobbins for each and commencing each at the end furthest from the handle. Sew in each section to the handle, tie and cut the ends. Now go the base of the umbrella and hang on 12 pairs of bobbins. Work one row in whole stitch and then change to the following pattern. Working from left to right, each row consists of: one whole stitch, two half stitches, one whole stitch, two half stitches, one whole stitch and

three half stitches, ending with one whole stitch. The edge is a straight edge, so change the workers at each end and twist the workers *only* after each change-over. Do not twist the passives after the whole stitches, as they will correspond to the lines on the pricking and join in at the top of the umbrella where the points of the folds are commenced. The spike is worked in black. Hang on five pairs of bobbins at the point. Work in whole stitch with straight edges on both sides and sew in to the base of the material.

Rear back leg

This can now be worked. The outline is the same as for the rest of the rabbit. The filling is also worked in the dark fawn thread and is the whole stitch and twist ground as for the tail.

Rear paw and back ear

The fillings for these are worked in the dark fawn thread (841) as for the rear back leg, working downwards in both cases.

Front paw

The fillings for these are worked in the pale fawn thread (842) using the same stitch as for the rear back leg and is worked from the centre of the body outwards towards the paw, where the threads are sewn in, tied and cut short. To commence this section of filling, the threads are hung on the first row of pins in pairs.

Front ear

The filling for this is worked in ecru, commencing at the tip and adding or losing threads as required using the same stitch.

Underbody filling

Eleven pairs are needed for this and ecru thread is used. The stitch is Dieppe ground and it is worked from the front paw towards the rear leg. Where the main part of the body will be attached, a pin is inserted and the workers twisted three times before passing round this pin and continuing the next row of work. This makes a false stitch into which the threads of the main body can be sewn without a real edge being formed.

Main body filling

This is worked in the pale fawn thread (842). Commence by hanging pairs in at the bottom of the front leg, and work in the whole stitch and twist ground as for the rest of the rabbit. Pairs are added

or lost as required and normal sewings are worked at the pinholes where the underbody and front arm join the main body.

Face and eye

Fifteen pairs of bobbins are needed for the face which is worked in pale fawn (842). Commence the filling at the nose and work towards the ears. The eye uses pale blue (827) and black for the pupil. Work the face ground until pin (a) is reached (diagram 50). Hang on two pairs of blue at this pin for the eye using Technique 9 (p. 26).

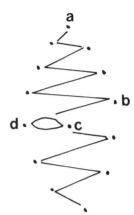

Diagram 50 Rabbit's eye

Work the eye in whole stitch, adding extra pairs as for Technique 8 (p. 25), until five pairs in all are being worked, and until pin (b) is reached. Now hang two pairs of black on a pin at (c). Weave one of the middle blue passives through these black threads to attach them to the rest of the work. Now work a tally out to (d). Do not put the pin in yet. Continue in blue from (b) in whole stitch and now work through both pairs of black. Put the pin at (d) and continue the eye in blue, losing pairs as in Technique 12 (p. 27) until only three pairs remain. The black threads are not used but can be tied and cut short. The blue of the eye can then be completed using Technique 17 (p. 28). Return to the main face filling and work it over the eye attaching it with sewings only at either end of the eye. Work sewings where the tips of the whiskers join the face.

Mr Bunny is now ready to be attached to the backing material.

10 Tablecloth

The centre section of this tablecloth was inspired by a Swedish 'Greek Key' design and the rest of the sections develop the theme, with the gradual introduction of more variety into the stitches, but keeping the essential concept.

There are no straight edges anywhere in the patterns as the threads round each edge pin of a section are joined together with the corresponding threads of the next section by slip-stitching them together using the same thread as the lace. There is, however, a twisted passive pair running along the outside edges of each section. Diagram 51 shows the assembly of the sections. The prickings are spread out from number 13 to number 17 (b). Each side pricking is marked to denote the position where it is joined to the corner pricking for that section. If it is required to use any of the sections as an edging in its own right, an extra pair of workers must be added to make a straight edge.

Dimensions
137 × 137 cm (54 × 54 in)

Materials required
3 spools Campbells 70 Irish Linen in white
64 pairs of bobbins

Section 1 (centre) uses 33 pairs of bobbins.
Section 2 uses 39 pairs of bobbins and has one repeat of pattern between the corners.
Section 3 uses 59 pairs of bobbins and has four complete pattern repeats between the corners.
Section 4 uses 61 pairs of bobbins and has three complete pattern repeats between the corners.
Section 5 uses 64 pairs of bobbins and has five complete pattern repeats between the corners.

Diagram 51 Assembly of tablecloth sections

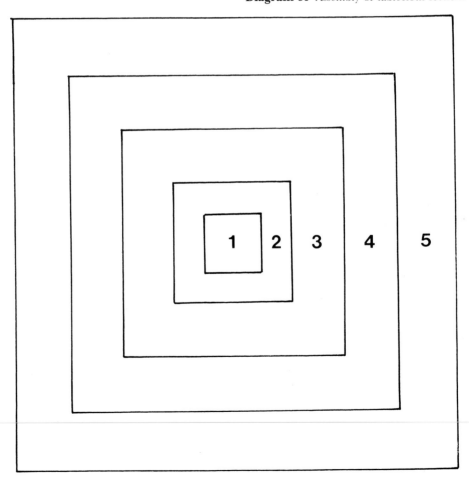

Figure 15 One quarter of the tablecloth showing the development of the design through the sections

Method of working

Each section is commenced at a corner using Technique 4 (p. 24). The 'Greek Key' design in the centre and section 2, and the following trails are all worked in half stitch. Do not work any whole stitches on the edges of these. Care must be taken when the 'Key' trails separate to make certain that the passives are evenly divided. If this is not done, there will be an incorrect number of threads at the end of that part of the trail. All the diamonds are worked in whole-stitch blocks except at the corners of Section 4 where some half-stitch blocks are indicated on the pricking. The basic ground is the Dieppe ground. Spiders are in- troduced in Section 3 and rose ground in Section 4. The edge is a Cluny one, twisting the workers once before working the outside pin, twice round the pin, and twisting both workers and outside passive pair once after enclosing the pin with a whole stitch. Finish each section as for Technique 18 (p. 28).

Pricking 13 Tablecloth centre (section 1)

Pricking 14(a) Tablecloth section 2 (side)

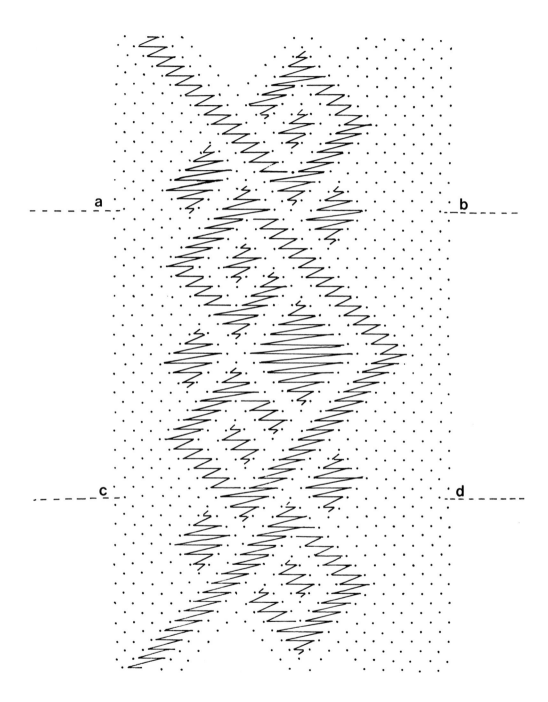

Pricking 14(b) Tablecloth section 2 (corner)

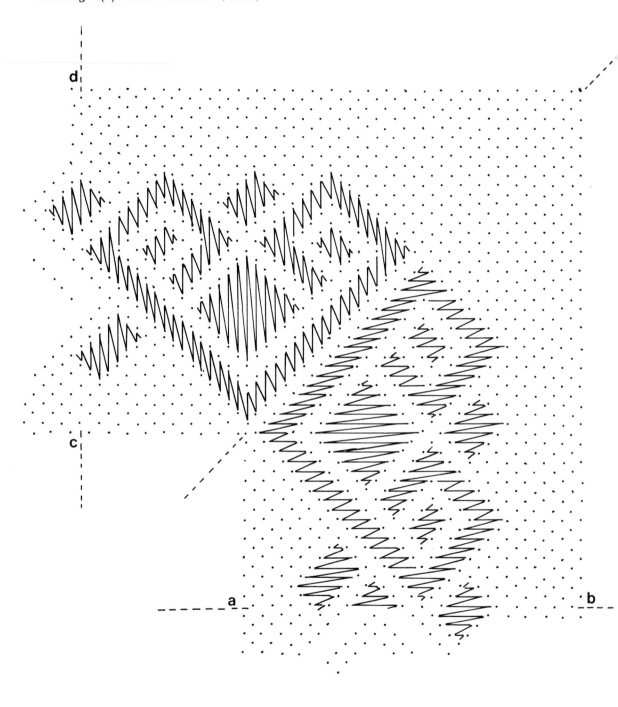

Pricking 15(a) Tablecloth section 3 (side)

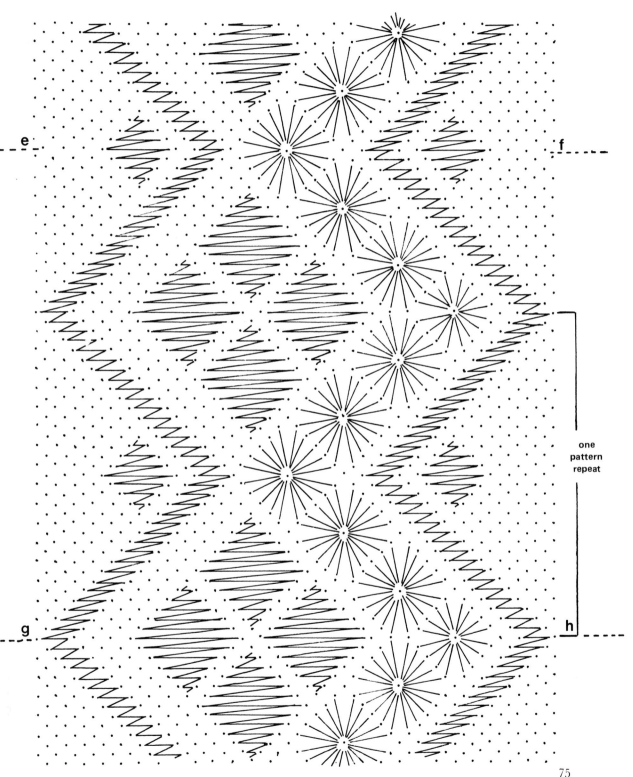

e

f

g

h

one
pattern
repeat

Pricking 15(b) Tablecloth section 3 (corner)

Pricking 16(a) Tablecloth section 4 (side)

m

n

one
pattern
repeat

j

k

Pricking 16(b) Tablecloth section 4 (corner)

n

½ st.

½ st.

½ st.

½ st.

½ st.

m

k   j

Pricking 17(a) Tablecloth section 5 (side)

o

p

q

r

one
pattern
repeat

Pricking 17(b) Tablecloth section 5 (corner)

11 Three napkin corners

These three Torchon lace patterns in different sizes are designed to complement the tablecloth pattern. They are worked in a slightly finer thread than that used for the tablecloth, but the patterns can always be enlarged to use a thicker thread or diminished to be used as a corner for a handkerchief.

Dimensions
Corner 1: 14 cm (5½ in) along foot side
Corner 2: 16·5 cm (6½ in) along foot side
Corner 3: 18 cm (7 in) along foot side

Materials required
BOUC Fil de Lin 90 thread in white
Corner 1: 28 pairs of bobbins
Corner 2: 36 pairs of bobbins
Corner 3: 37 pairs of bobbins

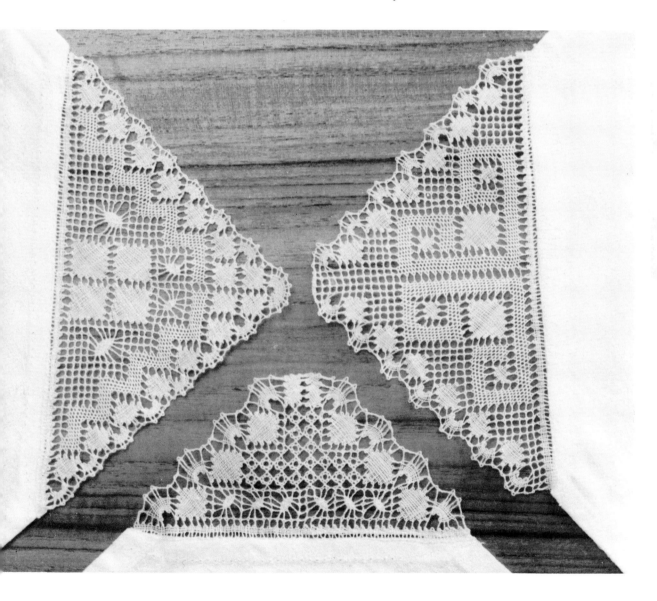

Figure 16 Three napkin corners to complement the tablecloth

Method of working

The following instructions pertain to all three corners unless specifically stated. The foot side has two untwisted pairs of passives and a straight edge using two alternate pairs of workers. The head side of each corner is a whole stitch Cluny edge, twisting the workers and passives once before and once after each edge stitch, and the worker pair twice round the outside pin. The basic ground is Dieppe ground. The 'Key' pattern and zig-zag trails are worked in half stitch, ensuring that the passives are divided evenly where the 'Key' pattern diverges. All the diamond shapes are worked in whole stitch.

Corner 1 has a rose ground filling. Also, when the point at the half-way line is reached, all the passives from the edge are incorporated in the whole-stitch blocks and carried across until needed in the second half. On Corner 3, one pin at the point needs to be worked twice (see Technique 22, p. 29).

Work in the direction shown by the arrow. Commence by working down the foot braid, adding in pairs on the inner side as per Technique 9 until the half-way stage is reached. Now the first half of the corner can be completed. At this stage, turn the pillow through 90 degrees and, starting at the point, work the other half, losing pairs into the foot braid as in Technique 14 (p. 27). Tie off at the end and leave one thread longer to attach the lace to the napkin material.

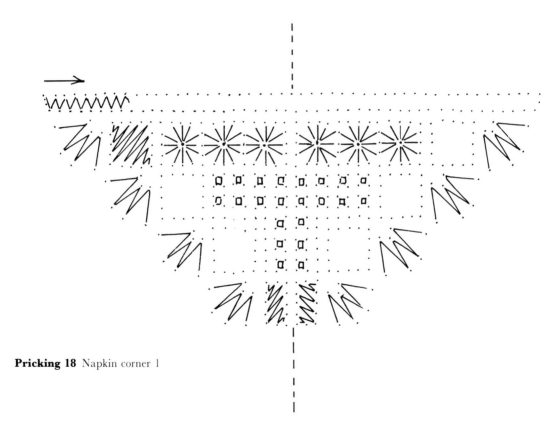

Pricking 18 Napkin corner 1

Pricking 19 Napkin corner 2

Pricking 20 Napkin corner 3

12 Badges and monograms

School and college badges or emblems make very interesting subjects for translation into lace designs. The pricking and instructions that follow give a shield outline and intertwined letters forming a monogram. In this case, the letters are the author's initials.

Monograms like this can be designed quite easily once the basic rules are understood.

1 Remember to draw the letters in reverse because the lace is always worked face downwards.

2 Always make sure that each letter passes alternately over and under the other.

3 The width of each letter must be kept the same round bends as on the straight, if not using fancy lettering.

4 Work the part of the letter that will be on top when the lace is finished before the section of the other letter which will be underneath.

5 Crossing points are worked as for Technique 23 (p. 30) unless the letters are very wide, when it is best to work a sewing at each corner.

6 The filling stitch is worked last, using normal sewings as for Technique 19 (p. 28) at strategic places on the letters so that they are attached to the filling but still stand proud of it when finished.

7 On pricking 21, the filling pinholes are omitted when they pass across the letters, in order to avoid confusion between the rose ground and the letters.

Dimensions
14×20 cm $(5\frac{1}{2} \times 8$ in$)$

Materials required
DMC Brillante d'Alsace 30 in the following colours: 816 (maroon); 350 (red); 947 (orange); 742 (golden yellow)
60 pairs of bobbins
backing material

The shield

Work the outside shield shaping first. Using the maroon thread (816), and seven pairs of bobbins, work in a plain whole-stitch braid. Commence at the top left-hand corner of the pricking and work round the entire shape. Pivot pins as in Technique 21 (p. 29) are worked at the sharp corners. Finish using Technique 15 (p. 27), but leave one outside thread uncut ready to attach the shield to the backing material.

The letters

Refer to diagram 52 for the letters. The letter 'S' is commenced first at point A using seven pairs of bobbins with the orange thread. The braid for both letters is a plain whole-stitch one. Work as far as point B using Technique 22 (p. 29) round the sharp curves. Now commence the letter 'V' with seven pairs of bobbins and the orange thread. Hang on four pairs at point C and add the other passives using Technique 8 (p. 25) until all the passives are included in the braid. Work as far as point D. The letter 'S' is now continued as far as point E working a braid crossing where 'S' and 'V' meet. The rest of the first half of 'V' can now be completed. Note that when point F is reached, the inside edge is changed to a straight edge for the rest of the braid to point G. Lose threads as per Technique 12 (p. 27) until only three pairs are left at G. Finish as for ending at a single pin (Technique 17, p. 28), but do not cut the threads too short yet or they may become untied when finishing the second half of the letter 'V'.

The second half of 'V' can now be commenced in the same fashion as the first half, hanging in the pairs at H and working as far as J. Work a braid crossing where 'S' and 'V' meet. The letter 'S' can

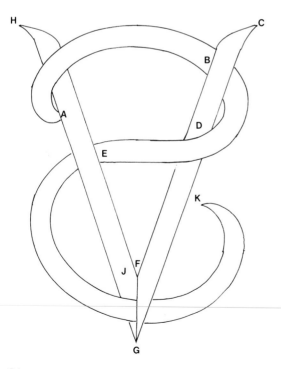

Diagram 52 Intertwined letters

Figure 17 V and S monogrammed badge to depict intertwined letters

now be completed, ending at K with a single pin. Remember to work sewings at the appropriate places and that pins are needed to be worked twice round the sharp curve. Finish the monogram by completing the second half of 'V'. Raised sewings (Technique 20, p. 29) are worked where the two halves of 'V' meet. By splitting the two halves of 'V' in this fashion, an appearance of a slot to pass 'S' through is given, thus intertwining the two letters more completely.

Completing the shield

The shield is completed by working a rose ground filling using 60 pairs of bobbins and the yellow thread. Commence at the top and work downwards. The many pairs of bobbins can be accommodated easily if the notes on the techniques for dealing with large numbers of bobbins are made use of.

This may appear to be a very complicated way of working letters, but the effect is worth the effort when the finished lace is mounted.

13 Fan

Although there are many fan patterns available, it is frequently extremely difficult to discover one that will exactly suit a particular set of fan sticks. Most of them are rather larger than this design and many take great numbers of bobbins to execute. This one is worked in small sections with filling stitches uniting them into one piece. By using curved stems and scrolls to separate the units completely, the widening radiating lines cause no problems in the ground stitches, and yet there is no appearance of the straight-lined geometric shapes that can occur with some patterns. It should be relatively easy to enlarge this pattern if it is required to adapt it to larger sticks or even to use it

Figure 18 A black fan using fine thread and worked in small sections

as a complete circular edging, because the design is very fluid.

Dimensions
a semi-circle of 13 cm (5 in) radius.

Materials required
DMC Rectors d'Alsace 60 in black (if the 60 thread is unavailable, 50 would be acceptable)
DMC Coton Perle 8 in black (310) for the gimp thread
17 pairs of bobbins

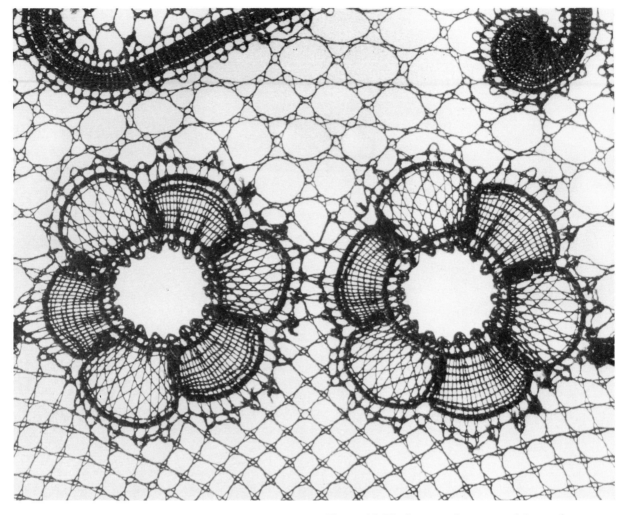

Figure 19 The fan: an enlargement of the two larger flowers

The Bruges flowers

The Bruges flowers are worked first. There is a slight difference to Technique 2 (p. 23) when commencing them, in that gimp threads are used to make an extra pair of passives as described in Technique 25 (p. 30). After hanging on seven pairs of bobbins with the thin thread and before working the first line of whole stitch, attach the gimp thread at the beginning of the flower by weaving one of the gimp pair through the centre threads as shown in diagram 53. This now makes five pairs for the centre block of whole stitch instead of four pairs of passives. When the first petal has been worked, weave the outside gimp thread through the centre block of passives, round the inner gimp thread and back again, before commencing the second petal.

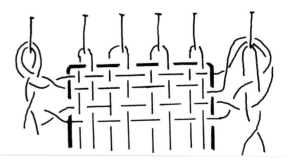

Diagram 53 Commencing a Bruges flower using gimp threads

88

Pricking 22(a) First half of fan

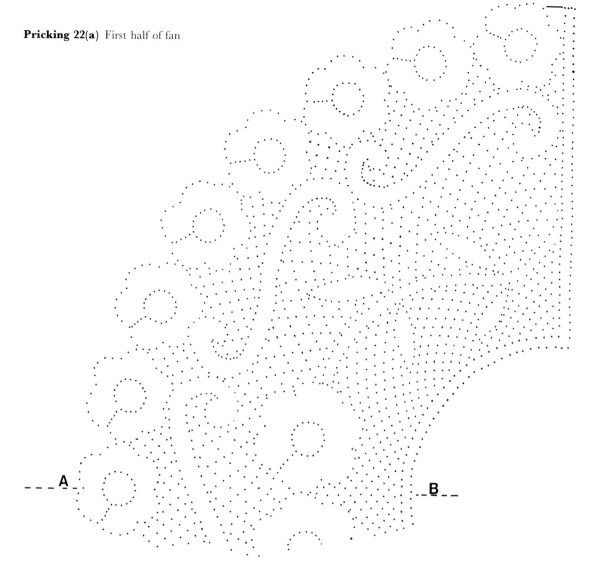

This movement is then repeated between each petal. When working the half-stitch petals, the two pairs of passives using the gimp threads are still worked in whole stitch without twisting them, although the worker pair is twisted after passing through them.

Outside braid
The outside braid is worked next using five pairs of bobbins. No gimp threads are used. Hang in two pairs at the tip of one of the end flowers and work a plait to join it to the end of the braid. These threads can now be worked into the edge braid. There is a straight edge at the very outside and three pairs of untwisted passives for the body of the braid. Twist the workers twice at the inside edge. Finish by

working a second plait at the end, sewing it into the last outside flower.

Now work the scrolls increasing to a total of six passive pairs as for Technique 5. Once again, though, the gimp threads are laid just inside the outer passive pairs and are worked in whole stitch in conjunction with the thin thread.

Stems
The stems are worked in whole-stitch braid using five pairs of thin thread and a gimp thread at each edge, making a total of six passive pairs. Start at the centre flowers and sew in to the edge braid.

Pricking 22(b) Second half of fan

Leaves

Each leaf commences at the tip (Technique 3, p. 23) and is worked in whole stitch, using Technique 8 (p. 25) to increase the threads to a total of six pairs of passives with no gimp threads. The workers are twisted between the centre passive pairs to form a vein.

Fillings

The fillings are worked last. There are three different grounds. The inner one is Dieppe ground; the centre is honeycomb ground; and the outer one Flemish ground. Note that when doing the latter, the larger sections are worked along the fan and the smaller sections are worked outwards. This breaks up the design and gives the impression that a fourth filling stitch is being used.

14 Wedding medallion

A wedding is always a special occasion and a lace memento can be a most acceptable gift. The names and date (Dennis, Veronica, 24 June 1961) on the original design have been omitted from the pricking, but correctly sized letters and numbers are given in prickings 24(a), 24(b), and 24(c) (pp. 95–96). When putting these on the basic pattern, remember to space them evenly and to place them back to front. If in doubt as to whether they have been correctly positioned, hold the pricking up to a mirror. The finished effect can be viewed, and any alterations in spacing etc. made.

Figure 20 Wedding medallion

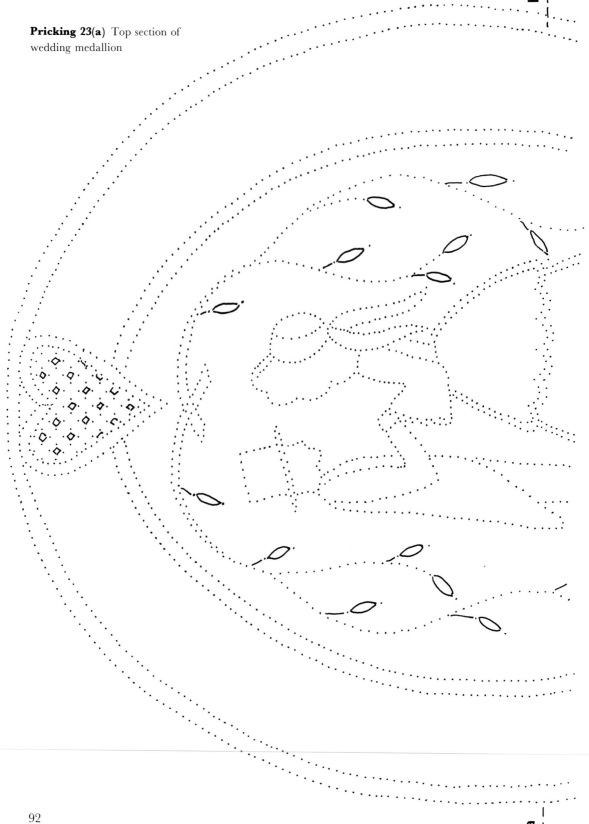

Pricking 23(a) Top section of
wedding medallion

b

a

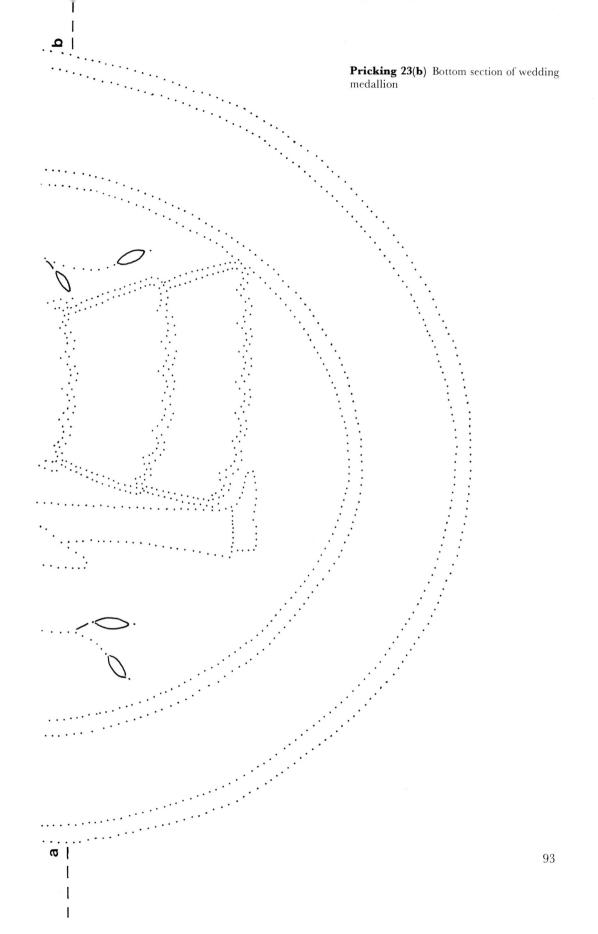

Pricking 23(b) Bottom section of wedding medallion

Dimensions
an oval shape 21·5 × 26 cm (8½ × 10 in)

Materials required
Retors d'Alsace 50 thread in white
Retors d'Alsace 30 thread in white
DMC Argent 10 (silver)
DMC Brillante d'Alsace No. 62 (variegated pink)
  and 369 (pale green)
Fine cream silk thread
41 pairs of bobbins
backing material

The heart

Commence by working the heart. The outside braid is in whole stitch, using four pairs of silver thread as passives and the worker pair in Retors d'Alsace 30. It is better to use a worker pair wound with ordinary cotton thread when using silver or gold passives because, when working sewings, metallic threads either crack or will not easily pass through small loops. The thinner, plain thread for the worker is almost invisible. The filling for the heart is worked in rose ground, using the pink variegated thread.

Outside braids

Next, work the two oval braids for the lettering. The outer braid has five pairs of passives in silver with a worker in white as for the heart. The worker pair is twisted once before and after working the outside passive pair and twice round the outside pin. The inner braid has one pair of passives less, and there are no twisted workers within the whole stitch.

Lettering and numbering

The letters and numbers may now be worked using four pairs of variegated pink for each letter. Try to finish the letter or number at one of the oval braids where possible in order to disguise the cut ends.

Leaves and stems

The leaves are tallies worked in pale green thread and they are joined to the stems with plaits. After working the end leaves, the plaits can be changed into ten-stick for most of the stem, gradually incorporating the stems that come into the main one and losing threads as in Technique 12 (p. 27), to avoid the stem becoming too thick. After the last leaf has been attached, however, the stem does widen into a whole-stitch braid. Use the technique for crossing braids (Technique 23, p. 30) where the stems pass over one another.

The girl

The figures are both worked in the 50 white thread. Only a brief description of the method of working is given. Work the crown of the hat in half stitch using ten pairs. Now work the two ribbons from the tips to the hat in whole stitch with straight edges on both sides, using six pairs of bobbins. The brim is worked in half stitch with two whole stitches and picots at the front edge. The dress sleeve is now worked, using eight pairs and half stitch, starting with a whole-stitch braid using two passive pairs (Technique 6, p. 25) and hanging in the passive threads evenly as for Technique 9, p. 26). At the inner edge of the elbow, the pins are worked twice (Technique 22, p. 29). The bodice is now worked in half-gauze ground using four pairs of bobbins and commencing at the waist. The edge braids of the crinoline skirt are done next. Use four pairs of bobbins. The sides have straight edges but the flounces across the skirt are plain whole-stitch braid. The filling for the skirt commences at the hem with 41 pairs of bobbins and is made up of the following sequence across each row: four half stitches, one whole stitch, four half stitches, one whole stitch, etc. The whole stitch forms a line to depict a fold in the material. The middle section contains 35 pairs and the top section 28 pairs. Do not tie and cut the threads for each section, but carry them across the braids, working sewings (Technique 19, p. 28) at suitable places and losing the pairs not needed for the next section.

The boy

He is not as complicated as the girl. Commence with the hat brim and work a braid using four pairs with straight edges on both sides. Hang on eight pairs at the top of the crown and work to the brim in half-gauze filling with straight edges. The coat is also worked in half-gauze ground. The sleeve needs seven pairs of bobbins and the main body of the coat 11 pairs. The trousers are worked in whole stitch with straight edges. The shoe needs seven pairs—two pairs of whole stitch for the sole and the rest in half stitch. Commence at the toe and sew in to the trousers. The hand and face are in half stitch, using the cream silk thread.

Pricking 24(a) Letters

Pricking 24(b) Letters

Pricking 24(c) Numbers

Figure 21 A Christening dress for baby: a lovely family heirloom for the future.

15 Christening dress

This is a very pretty dress for a baby and can be made as a family heirloom, as was the original. It is worked in Torchon lace with the pattern developing through the different sections and will fit a baby up to one year old.

Dimensions
46 cm (18 in) long

Materials required
90 BOUC Fil de Lin in white
114 pairs of bobbins
½ metre cream silk or Terylene material for lining
three small white buttons

Yoke

The yoke uses 32 pairs of bobbins. Commence at the neck edge of the rear opening using Technique 6 (p. 25). Work down the rear opening, hanging in pairs ready to work the main body of the yoke as per Technique 9 (p. 26). Turn the corner at the other end using Technique 7 (p. 25), and the yoke

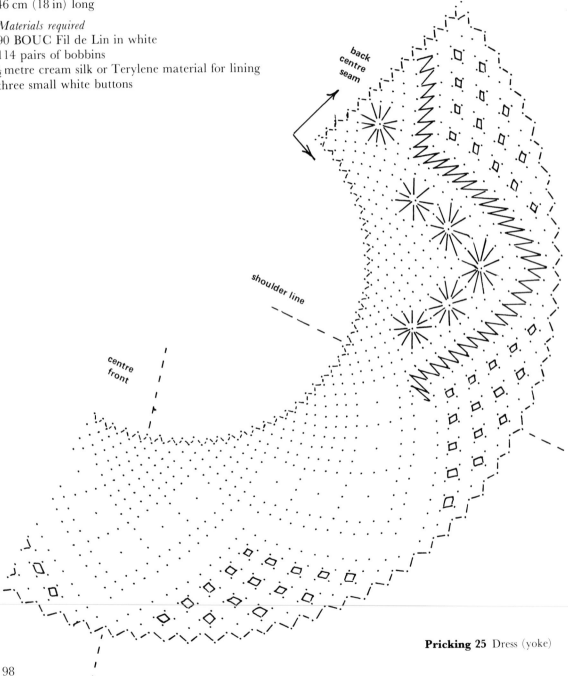

Pricking 25 Dress (yoke)

can now be worked. The basic ground stitch is: whole stitch, pin, whole stitch and twist both pairs once. This gives some elasticity to the finished lace which is needed in order to allow the wearer comfort of movement. Picots are worked at each pin on the neck edge and there are two untwisted passives on each edge braid.

The zig-zag trail is worked in half stitch, remembering to work a whole stitch at the pin where it joins the edge braid. On one side of the zig-zag is a rose ground filling whilst there are three-legged spiders on the other. Finish the yoke at the other back opening by turning a corner and losing the threads through the edge braid as in Technique 14 (p. 27).

Sleeve

This requires 52 pairs of bobbins in all. Commence at the underarm seam and work as for the beginning of the yoke until the corner has been turned. Add two more pairs to the edge braid for the sleeve hem so that there are four pairs of untwisted passives on that side and only two pairs for the seam where the sleeve is gathered into the yoke. Work the ground and the stitches between the three-legged spiders as: whole stitch, pin, whole stitch and twist both pairs once. Picots are worked at the hem edge pins, and threads are added at the shaped side when required as in Technique 9 (p. 26). After the shoulder line, they are discarded as in Technique 14 (p. 27). Finish the sleeve as for the yoke, but leave the two passive pairs from the shaped edge free and with a length

start

shoulder

Pricking 26 Dress (sleeve)

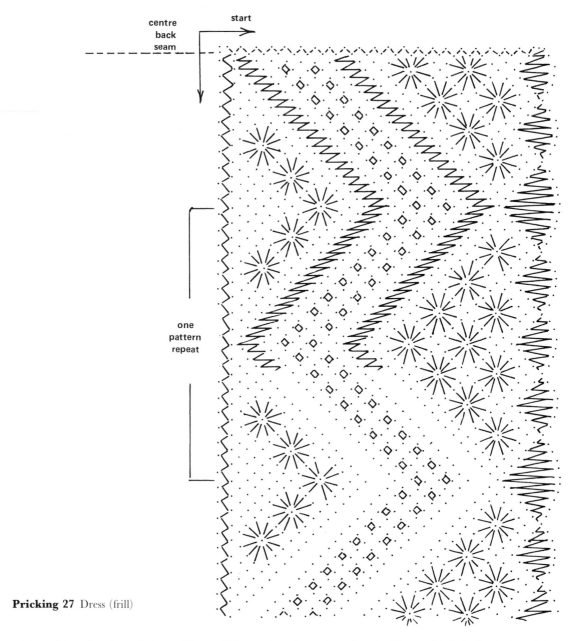

Pricking 27 Dress (frill)

of thread hanging from the lace. They will be used to gather up that edge to attach it to the yoke.

Frill

The frill needs 48 pairs of bobbins. Commence at the centre back seam and work the beginning as for the yoke. Once all the threads are hanging in from the centre back braid, the rest of the frill can be worked. For the whole-stitch blocks at the bottom edge, the workers are twisted once before and once after working the outside passive pair, and a picot

is made at the pin. The trail is in half-stitch and the basic ground is the same as for the yoke and sleeve.

Work 21 repeats of pattern plus the half-repeat at the beginning and the same half-repeat in reverse at the end, finishing as per the yoke. Leave the passives at the edge seam that joins the frill to the main sections of the dress free and with long ends to draw up the gathers of the frill. The total length of the frill is about 167 cm (66 in). That is twice the distance round the main sections of the dress.

100

a

b

e

f

101

Main sections

The four main sections of the dress are rather large and, therefore, the prickings for them must be joined together before they are commenced. Diagram 55 shows the assembly of the prickings. This may appear complicated at a first glance but it becomes more logical as the pieces are alphabetically united. The back sections each use 104 pairs of bobbins and the front 114 pairs. Edge braids must be positioned on the top of the front sections and down the centre of the back sections. The diagrams only show one side of each of the front and back sections. The other sections are worked in reverse, but, if the zig-zag design is to follow through in a continuous fashion right round the whole dress, it is necessary to replace that part of the pricking with the alternate reversed ones. Prickings 28(e) and 28(f). If necessary, the dress may be lengthened by making the large spider pattern deeper.

Each pattern is commenced at the shoulder using Technique 6 (p. 25). The side braids each have two pairs of untwisted passives. Pairs are hung in along the top as per Technique 9 (p. 26); the corners are turned using Technique 7 (p. 25) and the threads are discarded at the bottom (Technique 14, p. 27). When working the corners at the top centre of each section, it is better to leave the braid passives loose and to join in fresh ones for the braid down the centre. This is to allow the top to be gathered to the yoke using these threads.

Assembly

To sew all the sections of lace together in order to make the dress, a narrow buttonhole stitch is used, placing each section right sides together. This ensures that the seams are almost invisible and are also able to disguise any cut ends of thread. Firstly, join the shoulder seams and the centre front seam. Then the yoke can be attached to the main body of the dress. The sleeves can be set in now. Shirring elastic is threaded through the edge of the sleeve to give it a puffed-up shape. The centre back seam is joined only up to the bottom of the zig-zag pattern. Next, gather the frill evenly and sew it to the bottom of the main sections with the join at the centre back. A lining can be made out of silk, Terylene or fine cotton material to the required colour. The original was made out of cream-coloured Terylene material. This can either be attached to the dress at the neck, shoulders and centre back opening, or it can be a completely separate garment used as a slip. Make loops at one edge of the centre back opening and sew the small buttons on the other side to correspond with these.

Diagram 55 Dress: assembly of main sections

Diagram 54 Finished dress

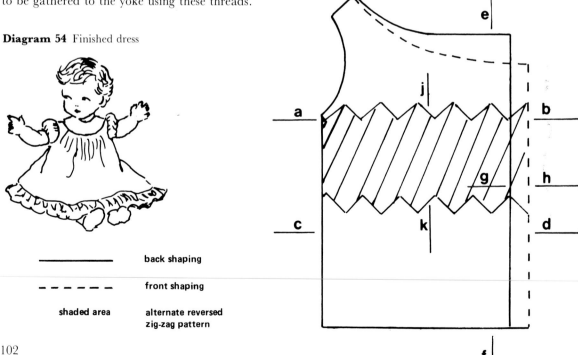

_____ back shaping

- - - - - front shaping

shaded area   alternate reversed zig-zag pattern

102

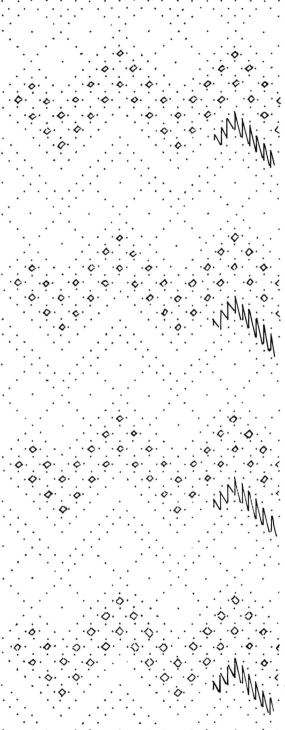

Pricking 28(c) Main section of dress (bottom)

c

f

e

d

Pricking 28(d) Main section of dress (centre)

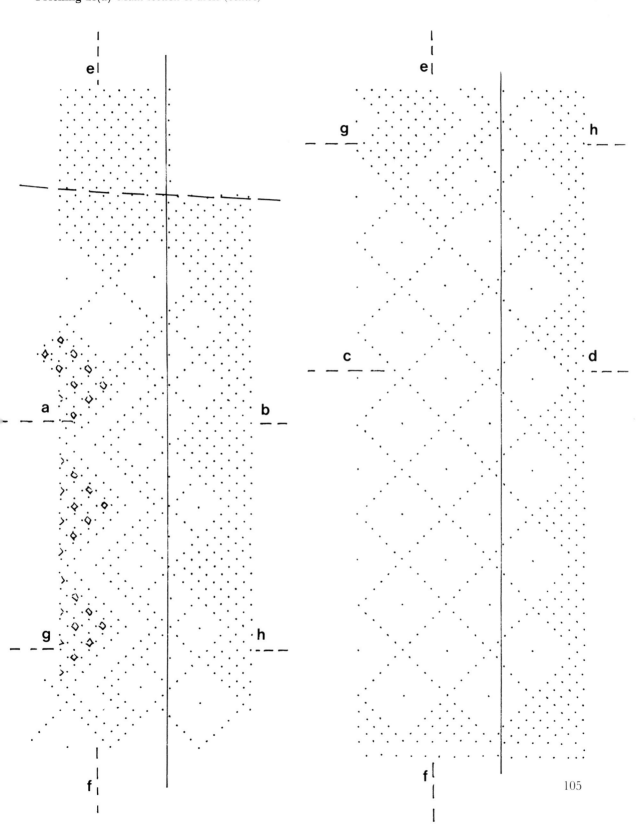

105

Pricking 28(e) Main section of dress (alternate centre)

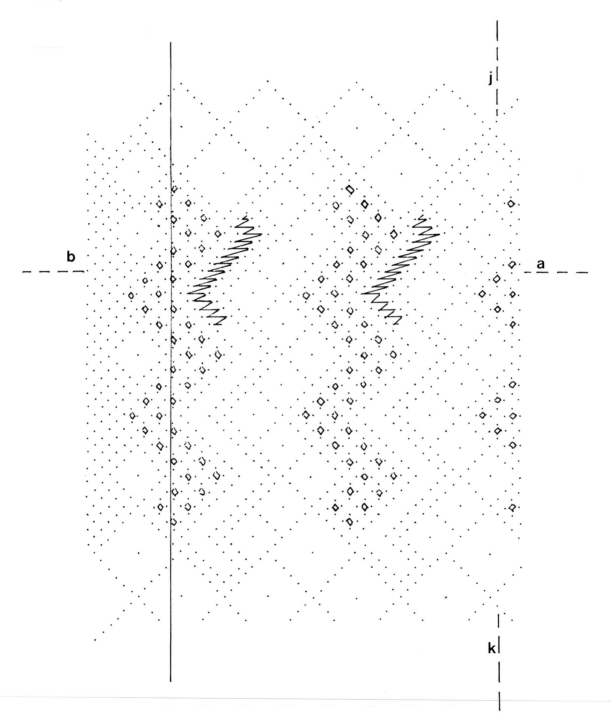

Pricking 28(f) Main section of dress (alternate side)

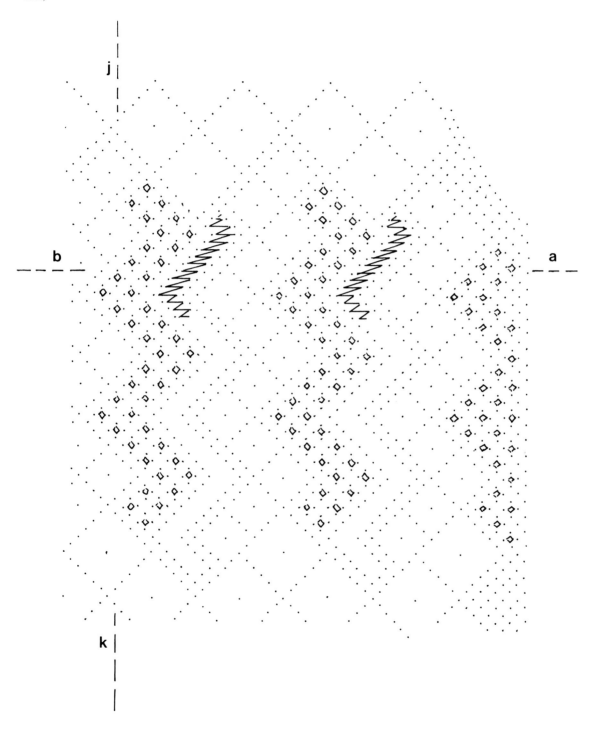

16 Ballerina

A television performance of the ballet *Swan Lake* gave the inspiration for this motif. The grace and movement of the ballerina was a challenge not to be resisted.

Dimensions
29·5 × 20 cm (11½ × 7½ in)

Materials required
DMC Retors d'Alsace 50 in white
DMC Argent 10 (silver)
backing material
25 pairs of bobbins

Skirt

As for all pictures and motifs, the foreground is worked first. This is the tutu skirt and, once completed, the trickiest part is over. Diagrams 56 and 57 show the method of working the fringe and a stylised cross-section of the tutu when completed. They will assist to clarify the instructions. It is not possible to put all the pinholes for the fringing on the pricking. So in order to lessen confusion, the lacemaker must determine the places for these when working the first two layers. All that she need remember is that the fringe must cover completely the braid beneath it. The braid base is in white thread and is worked in whole stitch. There are five pairs of passives in the top section and these are gradually increased to eight passive pairs for the bottom section. Pivot pins are worked at the front point to give shaping. The pair of bobbins that makes the fringe is wound with two threads of white and two threads of silver. Each braid is attached to the next with normal sewings (see Technique 19, p. 28) in order to make a solid piece of lace.

Bodice

Once the tutu is complete, the bodice can be worked. This is in whole stitch with straight edges, using the silver thread as workers and passives. Commence at the shoulders using four pairs of bobbins on each, and increase as in Technique 8 (p. 25) until there are a total of 25 pairs in both sides. The lacing effect down the centre is achieved by working: whole stitch, pin, whole stitch, with the workers from each side, to join the two halves together. When the waist is reached, the bodice should be sewn into the skirt, but this is very difficult as the particular thread used does not take kindly to being pulled through small loops. Therefore, it is better to use a needle and white thread to join these two sections after the lace has been removed from the pillow.

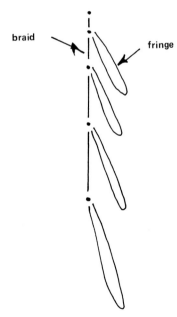

Diagram 57 Stylised cross-section of fringe

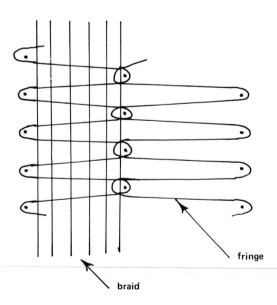

Diagram 56 Fringing stitch

Figure 22 Ballerina: the skirt, bodice crown and shoes in silver bring this dancer to life

Arms

Commence at the finger tips on a single pin as for Technique 3 (p. 23) with four pairs of bobbins, and work in half stitch with twisted whole stitch edge pairs, adding in extra threads using Technique 11 (p. 27) until a total of 12 pairs are in use. Finish by sewing in to the bodice working raised sewings (Technique 20, p. 29). Tie the threads and cut short.

Feet and legs

Commence at the toes, working in whole stitch and with the passive pairs wound with one silver and one white thread. As the shoe shaping gradually alters, take the silver thread off the bobbins and continue the leg in half stitch without breaking the white thread. Make sure that the edge stitches are worked in twisted whole stitch. Work the legs over the bottom layer of tutu fringing without making sewings and sew in to the braid.

Crown

This is worked round the top of the head. The two braids are in whole stitch using the white thread. The zig-zag sections are in silver plaits, using two pairs for each with picots at the tips.

Face and neck

Hang in threads round the top of the head using a total of 12 pairs of bobbins, and work in half stitch, ending at the bodice. When working these for the first time, use Technique 1 (p. 23) pin B to include them in the work.

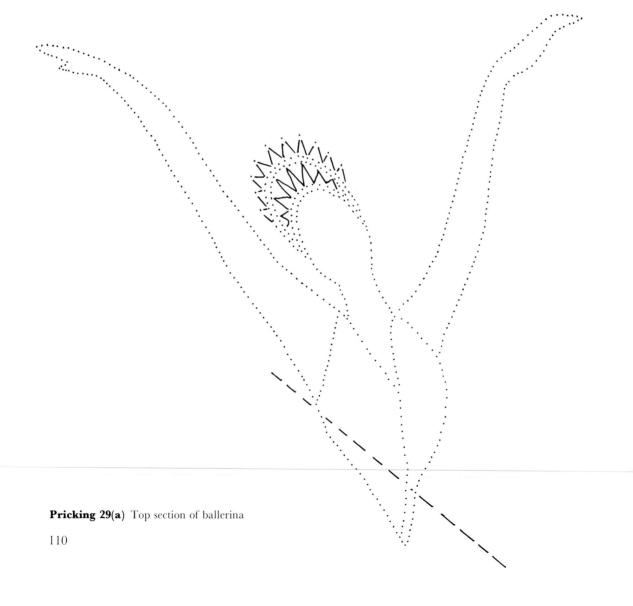

Pricking 29(a) Top section of ballerina

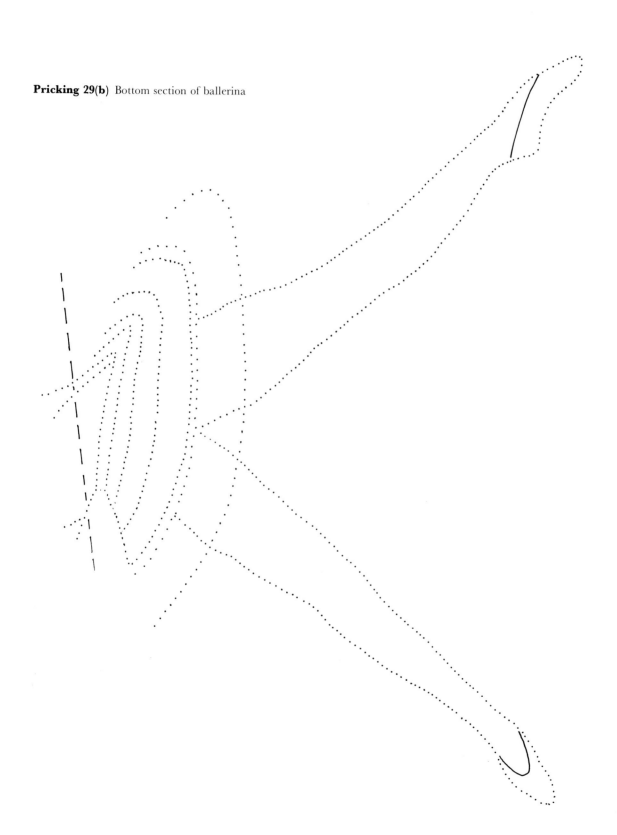

Pricking 29(b) Bottom section of ballerina

17 Winter scene

A Christmas card was the source of inspiration for this design. The snowflake effect is obtained from a Bedfordshire spider filling which matched the original lace framework. Unfortunately, although the framework design is a traditional Bedfordshire pattern, there is some query about copyright and,

Figure 23 Winter scene: the robin on his flowerpot appears almost in relief when seen in colour

therefore, the pricking for this has been omitted. The lacemaker wishing to work this picture must discover another suitable framework for herself. To give the flowerpot a little more substance, a small piece of tan-coloured felt, the same size, is inserted between the brown threads and the white snow underneath.

Dimensions
29×25 cm ($11\frac{1}{2} \times 10$ in) including the frame

Materials required
DMC Brillante d'Alsace 30 in the following colours: blanc neige (white); 349 (red – for the robin); 350 (red – for the holly berries); 434 (brown – for the flower pot); 801 (brown – for the robin); 310 (black – for the robin); (ecru – for the robin); 444 (yellow – for the Christmas rose); 369 (pale green – for the Christmas rose); 700 (dark green – for the holly); 320 (sage green – for the ivy)
tan felt
grey felt
70 pairs of bobbins

Ivy

The leaves are worked in half stitch from the base round each segment using pivot pins (Technique 21, p. 29) at the top of each point and working normal sewings (Technique 19, p. 28) for the veins. Finish at the point where the leaf was commenced. The stems are worked in ten stick after the leaves have been completed.

Holly

The berries are in whole-stitch blocks carrying the threads from one to another by twisting them several times. The leaves are worked in a similar fashion to the ivy leaves, but they are in whole stitch up the first side and, after working the pivot pin, the stitch is changed to half stitch down the second side.

Christmas roses

The centre of the flower is in half stitch using the yellow thread. The petals are worked in half stitch also, commencing each at the tip and sewing in to the centre. The petals for the bud are worked after the green base section which is also in half stitch. Two of the pairs from this continue to make a plait for the stem. When the base of the stem is reached, put in a strong pin to hold it in position and work a continuation of the plait up to the flower, sewing the threads in to the centre of this. The base of the stems can be caught into the snow when that filling is worked.

Robin

The wing is in whole stitch, commencing at the rear and using the dark brown thread with pairs of black passives to outline the feather markings. The eye is a black tally. Fuller instructions of how to work this are given in the pattern for the bird in the chairback motif (see p. 122). Now work the head and the top of the body in dark brown half stitch. The tail is worked as for the wing, with black passives to outline the feathers. The breast uses the red thread and is worked in half stitch, commencing at the bottom and sewing in at the head. Ecru half stitch is used for the underbody, starting at the front and sewing in at the rear. There is also a small section of half stitch in ecru for the top of one of the legs. The legs are in dark brown. Hang a pair of bobbins at the tip of each toe and twist them several times. Join these threads at a pin where the toes meet and work a plait for the leg to sew into the underbody.

Flowerpot

The top is worked first in brown thread and using half stitch. It is worked across the picture from left to right and the robin's toes are attached when those points are reached. The side of the flowerpot is in lock stitch ground and is commenced at the bottom of the picture, sewing the threads in to the top of the flowerpot.

Snow

This is worked in the whole-stitch clover ground, commencing at the left side and working across to the other side. Either carry the threads across the pieces already worked, or work the ground, guessing the position of the pins. Make sewings at suitable places to attach the foreground to the snow.

Snowflakes

The filling stitch for this is the snowflake or sunspot ground. Pairs are hung in at the top and the full complement of 70 pairs of bobbins are needed. Work the pattern as accurately as possible over the motifs already formed, with sewings at suitable places. Sew in the threads to the snow ground. It is better not to make sewings at the tips of the leaves as this can deform the leaves.

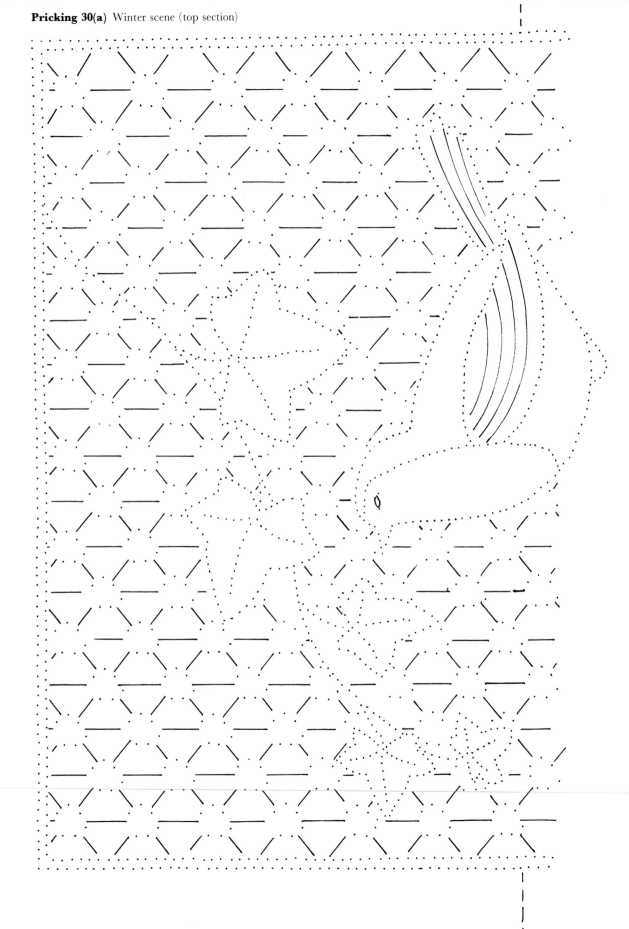

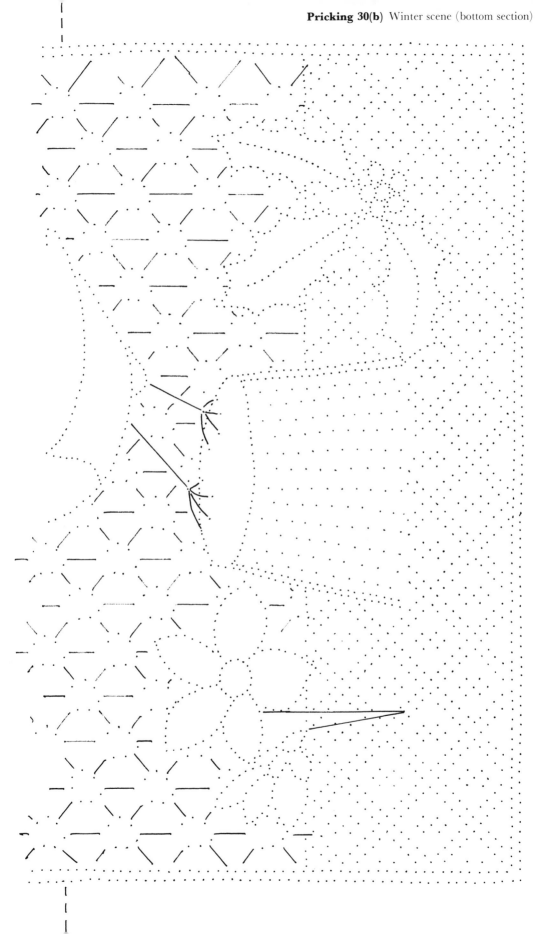

18 Windmill

Once upon a time, windmills were a regular feature of the English countryside. Unfortunately, most of them have now vanished but there are a few left. This lace windmill is a representation of a typical smock mill, and it was inspired by a local landmark near the author's home. A country scene was drawn as a background to give it a slightly more authentic appearance. The sails can be made to rotate if so desired.

Dimensions
26 × 20 cm (10½ × 8 in)

Materials required
DMC Brillante d'Alsace 20 in black (310)
Brillante d'Alsace 30 in 435 (light bown), 434 and
    433 (brown) and 801 (dark brown)
soft wire
32 pairs of bobbins
backing material
one black-headed berry pin to attach the sails to
    the structure.

Sails

Four of these are needed and they are worked in the black thread which is slightly thicker than the brown. The thin, soft wire is worked in conjunction with the outside black passive bobbin to give strength to the sails. The pricking shows one complete sail and the bases of the other three. Diagram 58 shows an enlargement of the top left-hand corner of each sail. Commence at the top right-hand corner as for Technique 6 (p. 25) and use three pairs of passives in each edge braid. Work along the top braid and hang in three pairs for the

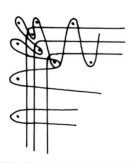

Diagram 58 Top left-hand corner of a sail

centre strut. Turn the corner and now work the sail. Working from left to right, each row is as follows: three whole stitches, twist the workers six times, three whole stitches, twist the workers eight times, three whole stitches. The workers are twisted twice round the outside of the pins. The centre pairs can be lightly pinned into place occasionally in order to keep them straight. When the base of the sail is reached, discard the wire and work a plait to the centre from each side. This leaves seven pairs of bobbins to work the centre block of whole stitch. Attach the sails to one another using normal sewings as this centre section is reached for each sail.

Structure

The roof is worked first using 32 pairs of bobbins wound with the light brown (435) thread. Hang the bobbins along the bottom of the roof and work towards the top. The first row is in whole stitch and the rest is worked in half stitch with one twisted whole stitch at each side. As the roof narrows, lose pairs as in Technique 11 (p. 27) and finish at the top with a single pin and four pairs of bobbins (Technique 17, p. 28).

Next work the railings. These need the black thread and five pairs of bobbins. They are worked across the structure from left to right. Hang three pairs at the bottom left-hand side and two pairs at the top of the left-hand side. The bottom edge is a straight edge with a change of workers, and at the top edge, the workers are twisted four times round each pin. Working from the bottom, the stitches are: two whole stitches, twist the workers four times, two whole stitches. The struts are also worked in black and each need four pairs of bobbins. They are worked in whole stitch, commencing at the bottom and sewing each into the railings.

The centre wooden section is now worked. Hang on 32 pairs at the bottom using the brown (433) thread. The doors and window are worked in half stitch and the rest of the work is in whole stitch, twisting the workers once after working each set of three whole stitches. Thus, the first row of work is: (three whole stitches, twist worker once) three times, two whole stitches, twist worker, nine half stitches, two whole stitches, twist worker, (three whole stitches, twist worker) three times. As

Figure 24 A windmill: the background scene drawn in black on the backing material gives realism

116

117

the doorway decreases in width, gradually incorporate the half stitches into the whole stitch pattern. When the base of the railings is reached, attach some of the passives with raised sewings. Five pairs of passives are discarded at this juncture, and the pattern is changed to the following: (two whole stitches, twist workers) five times, six half stitches, twist workers, (two whole stitches, twist workers) five times. Incoporate the half stitches into the whole-stitch pattern when the top of the door is reached. The top window uses the centre four pairs of passives as half stitches. Gradually disregard the twists between the whole stitches after this point and lose threads as for Technique 12 (p. 27). Sew in to the base of the roof.

The sides are each worked in a similar fashion. They both use 17 pairs of bobbins and sewings are made where they join the centre section. One side is worked in the dark brown (801) thread and the other in the number 434 thread. There are only two whole stitches, and not three, between each twist of the workers for the base part. Two pairs are discarded at the railings. The windows each use the centre four pairs of passives in half stitch.

Pricking 31(a) Windmill sail

Pricking 31(b) Windmill structure

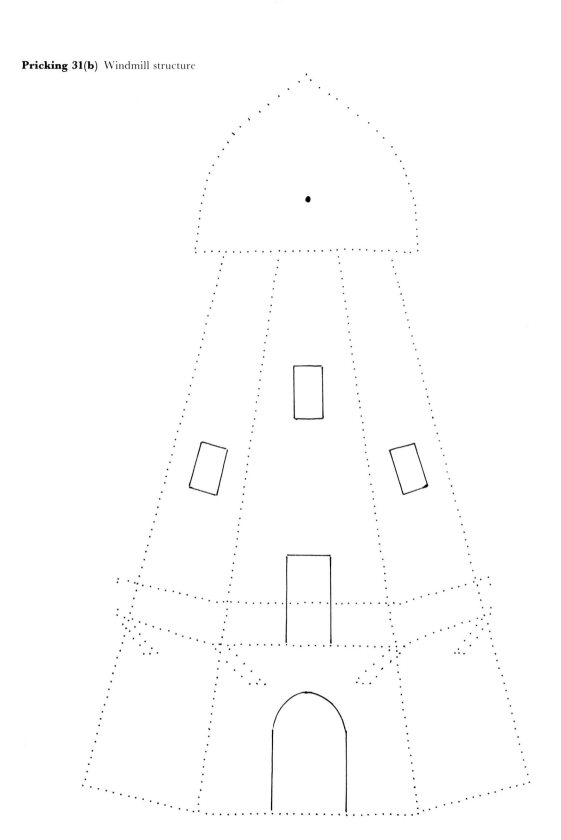

19 Chairback motif

In Victorian times, the antimacassar was very popular, but the covering of chairbacks for decoration and protection has become less popular these days with changing decor and furniture materials. However, this design shows that a room can be enhanced by using an appropriately coloured motif and, perhaps, making a feature of it. The adaptability of lace is also proved by the use of a pattern originally intended to be worked as an embroidery motif. Simple shapes like these Jacobean outlines lend themselves extremely well to the techniques of bobbin lacemaking. Because the pinholes are determined by the shape of the design, and not vice versa as in most of the traditional laces, these patterns make a pleasant change from the disciplines of geometric designs based upon graph paper.

The original motif was worked with a Dieppe ground to unite all the elements of the design after they had been worked, but the ground pricking has been omitted to obviate complications in working the lace. Diagram 59 shows the basic outline with the sections lettered in order that the various flowers and leaves may be easily identified. It is difficult always to state the exact number of bobbins used but, with practice, it is relatively simple for the worker to decide for herself the appropriate number. Only a brief description of the methods of working each shape is given as it is unlikely that a novice would be tempted to execute this pattern. When working it, remember that the bird must be completed first and then the flowers, with the leaves, tendrils and stems following. This ensures that the parts of the design in the foreground remain that way and that the other sections have suitable places to be attached with sewings so that the numerous ends of threads can be concealed. This technique is frequently seen in Honiton patterns but can be related to designs which have been scaled up from these. Hence, a lacemaker whose sight is not sufficiently good for

Diagram 59 Chairback motif: working diagram

120

Figure 25 Chairback motif

her to see the delicate fineness of the Honiton laces can still work patterns that are similar but on a larger scale.

Note that double pins and pivot pins are worked at relevant places on all the braids.

Dimensions
A circular motif of 22 cm (8¾ in) diameter

Materials required
DMC Brillante d'Alsace 30 in the stated colours
DMC Fil à Dentelle and Coton Perle 12 in the
  stated colours
Any suitable thread of like thickness and required
  colour for background (if desired)
Ready-made chairback or material to make same

Bird of Paradise

The wings are worked first, commencing from the tips and working towards the top in whole stitch. The outside feather of each wing works round the top and down the other side which enables the centre feathers to be sewn in tidily to this one. The threads used are: Brillante d'Alsace 30 51 (variegated orange) for the outside feathers; 947 (orange) for the next feathers; 350 (light red) for the centre feathers; 349 (dark red) for the inside feathers. The variegated orange should be arranged so that all the pale threads commence at the tip and they become darker as the feather progresses. The tail is worked from the tip inwards in whole

121

stitch using pale yellow for the outside feather; 444 (bright yellow) next; and 783 (gold) inside. The eye is now worked as a small tally in 433 (brown) thread. Leave the ends of this free to attach it to the rest of the head. The head and neck are worked in half stitch, commencing at the beak and using 947 (orange) thread. There is a twisted whole stitch at each side. Add pairs as required until there are sufficient. When the eye is reached, work a sewing at the commencement of this. When the end of the tally eye is reached, weave the brown threads through the head passives and leave them on top of the work to tie and cut later, whilst the actual tally lies underneath the head half stitch. The beak is worked in 433 (brown) thread from the tip inwards. Four pairs of bobbins are used. The top of the beak, is worked in half stitch and the bottom in whole stitch. This is to give a slight marking for the two sections of beak. The crown is worked last in gold Fil d'Argent à Broder 10. Each part is started at the tip and sewn into the top of the head.

(a) Tree

Coton Perle 12, 801 (dark brown) is the predominate colour although the worker pair is 801 (dark brown) Brillante d'Alsace. The dark green threads are gradually discarded and the workers are twisted on each row in the centre of a whole stitch braid. Sew the threads in to the tip of the bird's wings.

(b) Grass mounds

These are worked in whole stitch using two pairs of Coton Perle 12 906 (bright green); two pairs of 580 (sage green); and two pairs of 937 (dark green). The worker pair is a thinner thread in order that it tones in with the other threads but is not readily visible. It is Fil à Dentelle 954 (bright green). Having worked the mound next to the tree, carry the threads across to use for this.

(c) Leaf

DMC Fil à Dentelle is used in a bright green colour with a darker green pair as passives to show the

Pricking 32(a) Left-hand side of chairback motif

a

b

Pricking 32(b)

Right-hand side of chairback motif

123

vein clearly. Commence at the tips and work in whole stitch throughout, ending with a small plait to attach the leaf to the base of the tree.

(d) Flower

The threads needed are Brillante d'Alsace 30 996 (bright blue) and 91 (variegated blue). The outside shape is worked in a half-stitch block using the bright blue thread with a whole stitch and twist at the outside edges only. The filling is in the variegated thread. The only two fillings in the bottom part are in the whole-stitch and twist ground without using any pins (gauze ground). The filling stitch for the large upper section is half-gauze ground, working the untwisted threads downwards and the twisted workers across each row.

(e) Flower bud

Using the same bright blue thread as for the previous flower, work in whole-stitch braid, twisting the workers before and after the outside whole stitch. Work up one side of each petal; work a pivot pin at the top; and then in half-stitch braid down the other side.

(f) Flower

This is worked in a continuous whole-stitch braid, using Brillante d'Alsace 553 (mauve).

(g) Flower bud

Work this in exactly the same fashion as for flower bud (e) in the mauve thread used for flower (f).

(h) Flower

The outside braid and inside section are worked in Brillante d'Alsace 602 (pink). Use two pairs of passives only for the edge in a whole-stitch braid. The centre is a half-stitch braid. The filling uses thread No. 62 (variegated pink), and consists of three-legged spiders. Each petal's spiders are worked in a different direction to give interest.

(i) Bud

Using the same colour as for the previous flower, work the whole-stitch braid edges as in flower (h), making sure that the inner section is worked first and the tip one last. The filling uses the pink variegated thread and is worked in whole stitch and twist at every pinhole. The leaves at the base of the bud are worked in No. 700 (dark green) whole stitch from the tips inwards with twisted workers between the centre passive pairs.

(j) Acorn shapes

Use No. 801 (dark brown) for the cup in whole-stitch braid and No. 943 (blue/green) for the acorns. These are worked in a spiral whole-stitch braid commencing at the outside and working to the centre.

(k) Bud

Using the same thread as for the acorns, work in whole-stitch braid.

(l) Leaf

This is worked in a similar fashion and in the same thread to leaf (c) with the exception that the beginning is a ten-stick tendril which opens up into the leaf.

(m) Leaf

This is a whole-stitch braid edging in No. 700 (dark green) thread with a gauze ground filling of the same thread. There are no pins in the filling.

(n) Leaf

Work as for leaf (m) using No. 954 (pale green) thread.

(o) Leaf

Using the No. 700 (dark green) thread, work this in half stitch with a straight edge on the side that continues into the stem and one whole stitch and twist on the other side.

(p) Leaf

Work as for leaf (o) using the same thread.

(q) Leaf

This is a whole-stitch braid-edged leaf, using the No. 954 (green) thread. The vein in the centre is worked with two pairs of bobbins, working a twisted whole stitch.

The rest of the leaves are worked in a half-stitch ground with one twisted whole stitch at each edge in varying shades of green Brillante d'Alsace 30. The stems are worked in ten stick, using No. 801 (dark brown) thread and the tendrils are worked likewise using No. 320 (sage green) thread.

If a ground is not worked to attach all the different elements, the motif is now complete and ready for mounting, but care must be taken that each part is attached to the backing and that the shape is not distorted whilst this is being done.

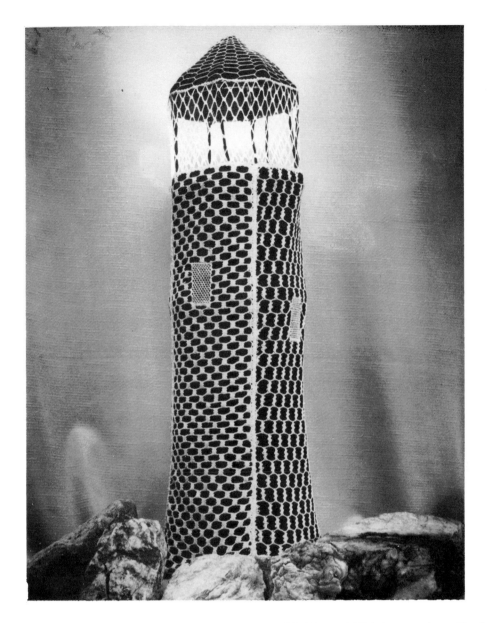

20 Model lighthouse

This is a table lamp with a difference. It is a
completely free-standing lighthouse with the light
only showing through the upper window. If a
flasher bulb were to be installed and rocks placed
round the base, it could make a realistic model.
The design was based on the Eddystone Lighthouse in southern England but it had to be
foreshortened slightly to avoid the height becoming too great.

Dimensions
61 cm (24 in) tall
20 cm (8 in) diameter at base

Figure 26 This model lighthouse makes a friendly
night-light for a nervous child

Materials required
four lampshade rings 15 cm (6 in) diameter
one lampshade ring 20 cm (8 in) diameter
two packets of florist's stub wires
reel of black insulating tape
½ metre of black felt
black thread or fabric adhesive
BOUC Fil de Lin 50 in white
54 pairs of bobbins

Framework

Bind all the lampshade rings with the insulating tape. Now bind the stub wires together in bundles of five to form lengths of at least 63·5 cm (25 in). Eight of these will be needed. Attach these eight lengths of wire to the rings as shown in diagram 60, making sure that they are equally spaced round the rings. The top of the wires will form the roof shaping. The black felt is now fitted round the framework omitting the section for the window. It is best to use the felt double in order to prevent any light from showing through in the wrong places. The roof felt can be made by using the pricking as a template.

Brickwork (section 1)

Each of the four main brickwork sections is worked as a different sampler with the half-stitch windows spiralling round the lighthouse. The window is positioned in the pricking for the first section but, for the other sections, only the number of pattern repeats before the window is given. The window shape is the same for all four sections and must be overlaid on the pricking for the other sections. Section 1 commences with 46 pairs of bobbins and is worked in the brick and braid ground. Start at the top right-hand corner (Technique 6, p. 25), but using three pairs of passives in the braids. Hang two pairs of bobbins at each of the pinholes marked with a circle on the pricking whilst the top braid is being worked in readiness for the main body of the section. Turn the top left-hand corner as in Technique 7 (p. 25). The main part can now be worked. When the window is reached, use the threads already in the work to form the half-stitch block with one whole stitch at either side. First, work one complete row of whole stitch to set the threads in position and end at the bottom of the window with two complete rows of whole stitch. Work 19 complete pattern repeats and then the bottom shaping. As the base of this pricking widens, four more pairs of bobbins are gradually incorporated into the work on each side. Finish across the bottom using Technique 14 (p. 27).

Brickwork (section 2)

The second brickwork section is worked in the Devonshire wall filling. Thirty-six pairs of bobbins are used to commence the work. Hang two pairs at each of the circled pinholes as for the first section. Six-and-a-half pattern repeats are worked before the window is placed and 20 complete pattern repeats before the bottom pricking is added. Four

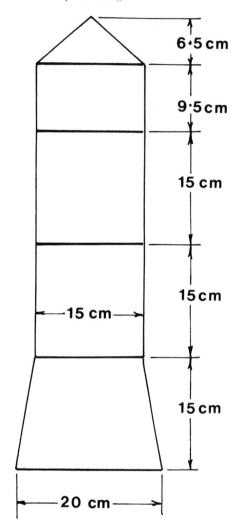

Diagram 60 Cross-section of lighthouse showing positions of lampshade rings

6·5 cm

9·5 cm

15 cm

15 cm

←15 cm→

15 cm

←20 cm→

extra pairs are added to work the half-stitch window and discarded when this is complete. Two pairs are added on each side as the base widens.

Brickwork (section 3)

The main body of the third section uses 40 pairs of bobbins and is worked in whole-stitch block ground. Hang two pairs of bobbins at the circled pinholes and one pair at each of the rest. Five pattern repeats are worked before the window is commenced and four extra pairs will be needed for this. Ten complete pattern repeats are worked before the bottom shaping and four extra pairs will be added on each side as the base widens.

126

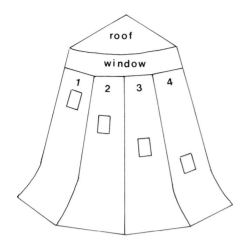

Diagram 61 Assembly of lighthouse lace

Brickwork (section 4)

The filling stitch for the fourth section is the pea with braid ground. Twenty-eight pairs of bobbins are used to commence this, hanging two pairs on each circled pinhole. Work 13 pattern repeats before the window is placed and eight extra pairs will be needed for this. Twenty-one complete pattern repeats are worked before the base widens and four more pairs are added on each side near the base.

Window

The window is worked round the lighthouse rather than vertically. It is the flower-centred braid ground and needs 22 pairs of bobbins. Commence

Pricking 33(a) Lighthouse brickwork section 1 (top)

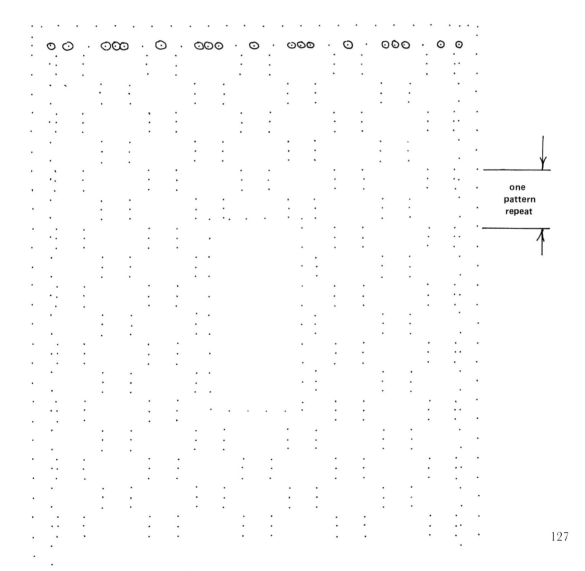

one
pattern
repeat

127

at the top right-hand corner with six pairs and work a plait across the top, hanging in the number of pairs as indicated on the pricking. Plaits are worked down each side. A total length of 51 cm (20 in) is needed before completing with a plait across the width of the work. Tie the threads but do not cut them too short. They can be incorporated better in this way when the join is made by oversewing them.

Roof

The roof requires 31 pairs of bobbins and is worked in the braided net ground. If two pairs of bobbins are hung on each pin at the beginning, the ends can be sewn into the loops formed by them when the whole-stitch braid at the end is complete. Thus the roof shaping is formed.

Pricking 33(b) Lighthouse section 1 (bottom)

Assembly of lace

Join all the side sections together with flat seams, overlapping the whole-stitch edge braids, but do not make the final join yet. Now sew the bottom edge of the window to the top of these sections and the outer edge of the roof to the top edge of the window (see diagram 61). The lace can now be placed on the finished framework and the final seams joined all the way down. The top and bottom of the window may need to be attached to the felt underneath and the bottom of the lace should be stretched and folded under the felt. It is then slip-stitched into position. The table lamp can now be placed inside the lighthouse. It is best if the lamp is below the level of the lighthouse window so that the bulb does not show when alight. It is recommended that a low-watt bulb is used.

Pricking 34(a) Lighthouse brickwork section 2 (top)

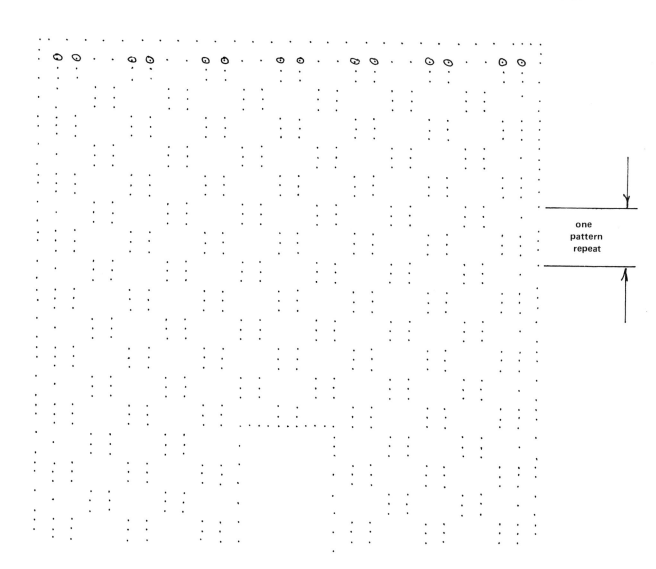

one
pattern
repeat

Pricking 34(b) Lighthouse brickwork section 2
(bottom)

Pricking 35(a) Lighthouse brickwork section 3 (top)

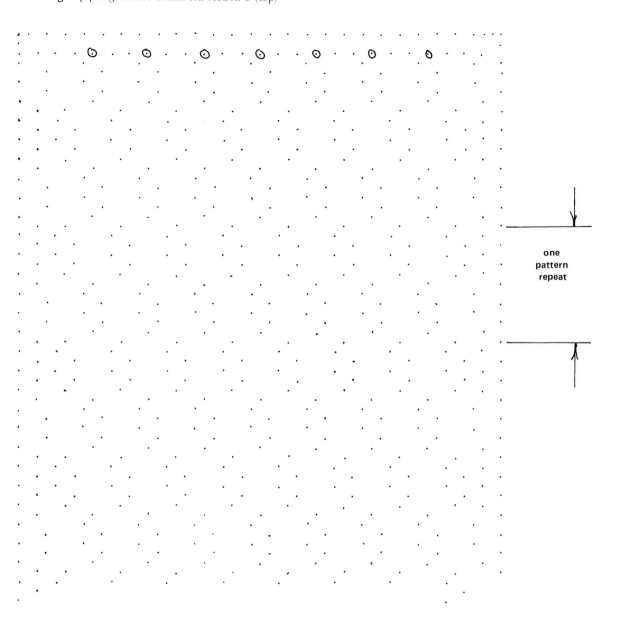

one
pattern
repeat

Pricking 35(b) Lighthouse brickwork section 3
(bottom)

Pricking 36(a) Lighthouse brickwork section 4 (top)

one
pattern
repeat

Pricking 36(b) Lighthouse brickwork section 4
(bottom)

Pricking 37 Lighthouse window

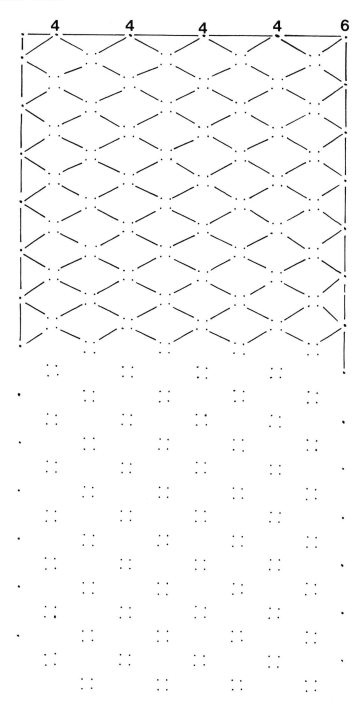

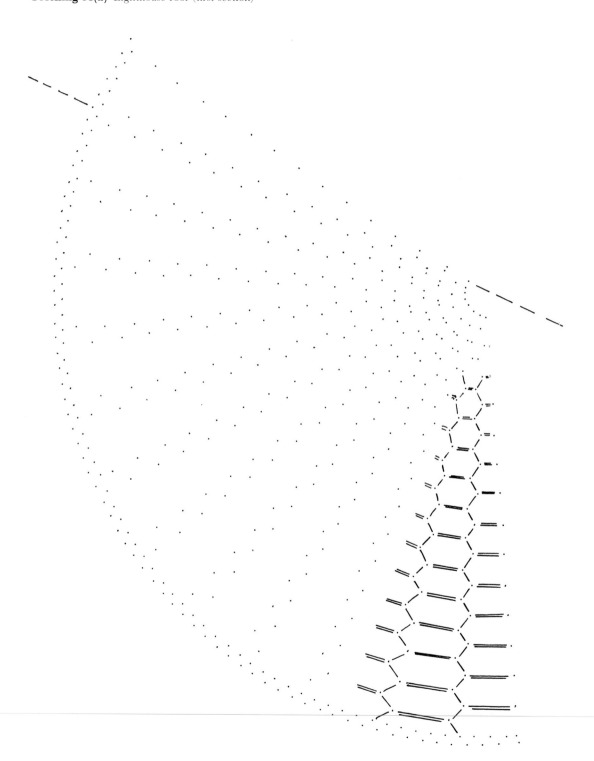

Pricking 38(b) Lighthouse roof (second section)

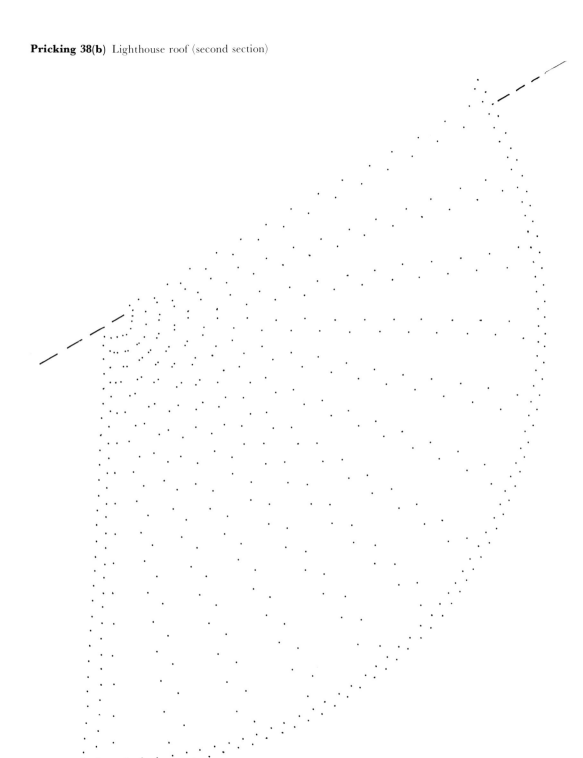

7 Designing lace pictures

Motives for designing

What gives a lacemaker the urge to try her own designing? This question has a multitude of answers and the traditionalist will usually reply with another question: 'What is wrong with the traditional laces and patterns?' Naturally, the answer to this is: 'Nothing'. They are truly beautiful but the fact that so many people have worked the same pattern can sometimes prove that familiarity breeds contempt. Some lacemakers find it monotonous to work always in the traditional white, black or ecru threads and there are others whose sight is not good enough to work with fine neutral-coloured threads.

First designs

How does a lacemaker know when she is ready to commence attempting her own designing? There is no hard and fast rule about this but the main guideline must be a burning desire to do so. It is best to learn to work the traditional types of patterns and stitches before attempting designing. The physical constraints of: 'Where does this thread go?' or: 'How many pairs of bobbins are needed?' must be able to be answered before the known techniques can be translated into a different type of pattern.

Inspiration

Where does the inspiration for new designs originate? There are many sources. Perhaps a television programme sparks off that gem of an idea or a chance remark by a friend. Newspaper articles, local landmarks, or a well-loved view may be other sources. What about photographs or pictures in books or even designs being worked in other mediums such as embroidery or crochet?

Some lacemakers have a yearning to work a particular design for many years before they actually do it and others may be dared to attempt the seemingly impossible by another lacemaker.

Once an idea has been formulated, the use for the end product must be decided upon. It is no good working a piece of lace and then wondering what to do with it. A tablecloth must be large enough and of the correct shape to cover the table and the position of a table lamp must be determined. The colouring of a picture and its backing material is resolved by the wall on which it is to be hung.

Drawing pictures

One of the easiest types of design to attempt is a simple picture and it is not even necessary to be able to draw to do this, although, of course, life is made easier if it can be sketched out directly. First of all, decide on the size of the finished picture and where it will be placed when completed. Now, find a suitable picture from which to copy the outline. Perhaps this will be in a child's book or a poster or on an embroidery pattern. The shape must be simple. Embellishments are not essential or even desirous.

If the original picture is the wrong size and the outline cannot be traced directly, there are various methods of obtaining the required dimensions.

1 By using a pantograph or 'Sketchograph'.

2 By using a sophisticated reproduction machine as found in some business establishments, although these are not readily available to the majority of people.

3 By using squares. This method is taught in many schools.

This last method is very effective and relatively

simple to execute. A grid is drawn on tracing paper and placed over the original picture. Then, either by using graph paper or by drawing another grid with lines nearer or more distant than on the original one, the outline of the picture can be transferred, square by square, to make it the correct size.

Method of working

Although the outline of the picture is now prepared, it is still not time to commence actual lacemaking. Two things must first be decided. Is the picture to be worked all in one piece, or will there be a braid outline? If the latter, what filling stitches must be used to obtain the desired effect? Having decided the answers to these questions, the colour, if any, of the picture must be chosen and the thickness of thread to be used. Remember that a whole-stitch braid looks neater if a fine thread is used with a greater number of bobbins, unless an open effect is wanted.

There are two methods of obtaining the appearance of depth to a flat picture. Coloured threads may be used with the deeper colours to depict rear sections, or judicious use of a combination of stitches in one colour can achieve a similar result.

It must also be remembered that the picture will be reversed when taken off the pillow. It if has lettering, the outline must be drawn on tracing paper and then placed upside down on the pillow. One lacemaker, when working her first design, forgot this and produced some magnificent and wonderfully weird lettering on her picture. Nor could it be shown on the wrong side as she had carried her threads across the lettering. So, be warned!

Commencing the lace

Many people do not know where to commence the lace. Imagine that the object of the drawing is three-dimensional. What is the nearest point to the onlooker? If it is the nose of an animal, that is where the lace is commenced. If some branches of a tree are in front of the trunk, they must be worked first. When the front section has been worked, the part of the imaginary three-dimensional picture that is directly behind this is worked, and so on. The different sections of lace are joined with sewings and the threads carried across the parts already worked. This is unless the front pieces are worked in open lace stitches and are solid in reality. The rear section, obviously,

must not then be seen. In that case, threads of the rear sections must be sewn in, tied and cut short at the edge of the front sections.

It should now be possible to design and work the first simple picture. From that jumping-off platform, the designs can become more and more elaborate and ambitious and before she really knows it, the novice designer has become an expert!

Thread comparisons

These thread comparisons are intended to assist the designer when deciding which threads to use. They are all approximate, and other threads are available which have not been included here. If a lacemaker is not sure whether a particular thread is correct for a certain pattern, she should work a small section of whole stitch. If the material so formed is close-knit and firm, that thread is the correct one to use. If it is loose, a thicker thread is required; if the threads appear too cramped, a thinner thread is indicated.

Very heavy coarse work
(and use as gimp threads)
20 and 40 Crochet cotton
35 two-cord Swedish linen
35 Campbells Irish linen
5 and 8 DMC Coton Perle

Heavy work
(household linens, most Torchon designs, Russian tape laces, heavy beds/Maltese, also gimp threads with fine work)
70 two-cord Campbells Irish linen
50 two-cord Swedish linen
50 two-cord BOUC (Belgian) linen
50 and 60 DMC Cordonnet
100 three-cord Barbours linen
60 Coats Crochet cotton
12 DMC Coton Perle

Medium work
(Finer household linens, Torchon, Russian tape and Beds/Maltese)
100 DMC Cordonnet
80 DMC Cordonnet
100 two-cord Barbours linen
100 two-cord Campbells linen
90 and 100 BOUCS (Belgian) linen
80 and 90 two-cord Swedish linen
70 DMC Fil à Dentelle
30 silk

Fine work

(coarse Bucks Point, fine Torchon, Beds/Maltese)
100 two-cord Swedish linen
30 DMC Brillante d'Alsace
30 and 40 DMC Retors d'Alsace
30 Coates Italian
50 Filato di Cantur
60 Trident
100 two-cord BOUC (Belgian) linen
fine silk

Very fine work

(Bucks Point)
90 Coats Italian
100 and 120 Copley Marshall
50 and 60 DMC Retors d'Alsace
120 and 140 two-cord BOUC (Belgian) linen
150 Unity cotton
very fine silk

8 Helpful hints for better lacemaking

1 Do not let the work become grubby. Clean hands are essential, so is the frequent laundering of worker cloths and pillow covers.

2 If you have the time, make two pillows – one bolster and one flat. The bolster is better for long, straight lengths of lace and the flat pillow for small pieces and mats.

3 Always use worker cloths across the whole width of the pillow in order to cover the pattern and any work already completed. The bobbins will stay in place more easily this way.

4 Make sure that the pillow is rock hard or the pins will not retain their positions. Add more stuffing at intervals if necessary.

5 Wind the bobbins evenly. The slip knot may not hold if it is on an unevenly wound bobbin. Some bobbins and threads require double slip knots.

6 Always keep the length of thread the same as the length of the bobbins in use. If the thread is shorter, the work will not lie flat on the pillow and, if longer, the threads and bobbins can easily become tangled.

7 Linen thread holds its shape better than cotton thread. It is false economy to save on the cost of thread.

8 Keep the tension even by making sure that the threads are pulled firmly after each stitch. Accuracy is more important than speed.

9 Check the positions of the passives at frequent intervals when working a block of cloth stitch in order to keep them evenly distributed.

10 Always work in a good light to prevent the pins from casting shadows on the work.

11 Make sure that the pinholes in the pattern are true. Any pins inserted out of alignment cause a distortion of the lace and untidy work.

12 Do not use ordinary dressmaking pins as these rust if left in the work for any length of time and mark the lace.

13 Push the pins at least half way into the pillow – not just the tips.

14 Put the edge rows of pins at an angle so that they can hold the tension of the work. The edge may shrink inwards if this is not done.

15 When working long lengths of lace, leave at least 5 cm (2 in) of pins in the work so that the threads and weight of the bobbins do not pull the work out of shape.

16 Never pull the pins out at an angle or too many at a time. The work will pull out of shape if this is done.

17 When undoing incorrect work, always untwist the threads before taking out the pins. Never take out a group of pins and then hope to untwist the threads.

18 Take out the edge pins last of all.

19 Berry pins are very useful for edge pins as they are stronger than brass ones. But do not leave them in for any length of time (for example, six months).

20 Try to leave a piece of work overnight before removing the pins. This allows the thread to 'set' into shape.

21 Always pin the pattern as near as possible to the centre of the pillow.

22 Finally, never be satisfied with second best. Lace can easily be undone and most proficient lacemakers are as quick at undoing their work as they are at making lace!

Bibliography

COLLIER, Ann, *Creative Design in Bobbin Lace*, Batsford, 1982

COOK, Bridget M. and STOTT, Geraldine, *Book of Bobbin Lace Stitches*, Batsford, 1980

COOK, Bridget M. and STOTT, Geraldine, *Introduction to Bobbin Lace Stitches*, Batsford, 1983

DYE, Gillian, *Bobbin Lace Braid*, Batsford, 1979

LUXTON, Elsie, *Technique of Honiton Lace*, Batsford, 1979

LUXTON, Elsie, *Honiton Lace Patterns*, Batsford, 1983

MAIDMENT, Margaret, *Manuel of Hand-made Bobbin Lace Work*, Batsford, 1983

NOTTINGHAM, Pamela, *Technique of Bobbin Lace*, Batsford, 1976

NOTTINGHAM, Pamela, *Technique of Bucks Point Lace*, Batsford, 1981

NOTTINGHAM, Pamela, *Bobbin Lace Making*, Batsford, 1983

NOTTINGHAM, Pamela, *Technique of Torchon Lace*, Batsford, 1979

STOTT, Geraldine and COOK, Bridget M., *100 Traditional Bobbin Lace Patterns*, Batsford, 1982

List of suppliers

UK

E. Braggins & Sons
26–36 Silver Street
Bedford
Bedfordshire

Mace & Nairn
89 Crane Street
Salisbury SP1 2PY
Wiltshire

Win Sargent
Cottage Crafts
3 High Heavens Wood
Marlowe Bottom, Bucks

D. J. Hornsby
149 High Street
Burton Latimer
Kettering, Northants

Ye Honiton Lace Shoppe
44 High Street
Honiton
Devon

Christopher Williams
23 St Leonards Road
Bournemouth
Dorset BH8 8QL
(old and new lace books)

Bryn Phillips
'Pantglas'
Cellan
Lampeter
DYFED SA48 8JD
(beautiful bobbins)

Christine & David Springett
21 Hillmorton Road
Rugby, Warwickshire
(modern versions of traditional
bobbins)

George White
Delaheys Cottage
Thistle Hill
Knaresborough
North Yorks

USA

Arbor House
22 Arbor Lane
Roslyn Hights
NY 11577

Baltazor, Inc.
3262 Severn Avenue
Metaire, LA 7002

Berga-Ullman, Inc.
P.O. Box 918
North Adams, MA 01247

Frederick J. Fawcett
129 South Street
Boston, MA 02130

Happy Hands
3007 S. W. Marshall
Pendleton, OR 97108

Lace Place de Belgique
800 S.W. 17th Street
Boca Raton, Fl33432

Lacis
Antique Lace & Textiles
2150 Stuart Street
Berkeley, CA 97705

Robin & Russ Handweavers
533 N. Adam Street
McMinnville, OR 97128

Robin's Bobbins
Rte. 1—Box 294A
Mineral Bluff, GA 30559

Osma G. Tod Studio
319 Mendoza Avenue
Coral Gables, FL 33134

Van Sciver Bobbin Lace Supply
310 Aurora Street
Ithaca, N.Y. 14850

The Unique and Art Lace Cleaners
5926 Delmar Boulevard
St. Louis, MO 63112

The World in Stitches
82 South Street
Milford, N.H. 03055

Or your local bookseller

Index